TEAMWORK

Interactive tasks to get students talking

Jason Anderson

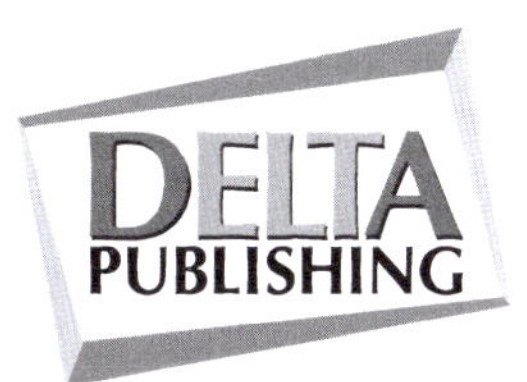

Contents

	Levels	Topic Areas	Language Focus	Quick Summary	Supplementary Activity
11 **Raining Cats and Dogs** *Page 46*	Upper int. Advanced	Idioms and proverbs; history / traditions	Past simple; expressing habitual past actions (*used to, would*)	After studying some common idioms in English, students play 'Call my Bluff' in teams, to try to guess the true origins of these idioms.	**Revision Activity:** Students analyse and correct mistakes in the form and usage of the idioms from the lesson.
12 **Stabbed in the Back** *Page 50*	Upper int. Advanced	Crime (murder); courts & trials, love & affairs	Past simple, past continuous; question forms; expressing emotion; agreeing and disagreeing	Students prepare for and act out all the parts in an exciting murder trial. Whole class role-play.	**Trial Report:** Students work in teams to write a brief article, reporting the details of the trial for a national newspaper.
13 **Survivor** *Page 54*	Intermediate Upper int. Advanced	Survival; the environment; travel	Conditional structures; future forms (*going to, will*); agreeing and disagreeing	Decisions Maze Activity: Teams of students work together to survive on and escape from a desert island.	**Group Discussion:** Students compare the different routes they took through the maze, and speculate on other, now hypothetical options.
14 **Front Page News** *Page 58*	Intermediate Upper int. Advanced	Newspapers, journalism, football & sport; flying & airports	Question forms; reported speech; tabloid news register	Teams take a front page tabloid scandal all the way from interviewing the protagonists at a press conference to completing the front page of the finished paper.	**What They Said:** Students focus attention on reported speech by completing sentences based on the interviews from Front Page News.
15 **Hungry for Haiku** *Page 62*	Upper int. Advanced	Poetry; places / geography; rhythm in language	Describing places, things and people; word order in sentences	After studying the rules of Japanese Haiku poetry, students try to order word cards to complete haiku poems, then they go on to write their own haiku.	**Haiku Classroom Poster:** Teams create posters based on the Japanese haiku poems that they have created. Group project task.
16 **Great Inventions** *Page 66*	Intermediate Upper int. Advanced	Inventions; communication; science & technology; media	Passive voice; superlative adjectives; infinitive of purpose	Jigsaw Communication Task: 3 texts about the history of 3 recent communication inventions: the internet, mobile phones and faxes.	**But When? Quiz:** Teams match dates with inventions. **Family Fortunes:** Teams play the popular TV game show in class.
17 **Natural Born Killers** *Page 72*	Upper int. Advanced	Animals, nature, the environment	Superlatives; asking questions; giving advice; reporting statistics	Teams of students get 1 of 4 fact files on different 'killer' animals. They then become experts and answer questions from other teams about their animals.	**Amazing Animals Quiz:** Students work in teams to decide which of 10 amazing facts about animals are true and which are false.
18 **"It's the Way I Tell 'em!"** *Page 78*	Intermediate Upper int. Advanced	Stories / jokes; humour; culture and cultural stereotypes	Present simple in jokes; direct speech; spoken discourse markers in jokes	Students in teams analyse the 'ingredients' of a good joke, then go on to practise and tell their own joke, getting the biggest laugh that they can.	**Joke Race:** Two teams of students race to communicate jokes and write them on the board. But they can only whisper.
19 **What Happened Next?** *Page 82*	Intermediate Upper int. Advanced	Storytelling; cars; mistakes; crime and law	Narrative tenses; *will / might* for prediction; expressing opinion; agreeing and disagreeing	Teams of students try to agree on what happened next at several stages in an amusing short story, then they compare their predictions with the original story.	**What Happened Next:** Group discussion, encouraging students to retell stories about mistakes they made in their past.
20 **The Ghost of the Séance** *Page 86*	Intermediate Upper int. Advanced	Crime / detective stories; houses & furniture	Grammar revision; narrative tenses esp past continuous; *there was / were* for description	Students try to identify grammar mistakes to win clues that will help them to solve a complex Sherlock Holmes murder mystery.	**End of Term or Christmas Party Suggestions:** How to turn the Ghost of the Séance into a whole school team activity.

1 Dreams Can Come True: Teacher's notes

Topic focus Sleep and dreams; Psychoanalysis

Grammar / Functional focus Making deductions (*You might be..., This suggests ...*); Making suggestions (imperative, *should*, etc.)

Level / Number of students Intermediate to Advanced / Minimum three students

Time 45–55 minutes (Extension 10 minutes)

Preparation

Copy and cut up texts A–D (1 per student). Use three texts in smaller classes of below ten students.

1 Suggested lead-in

Pre-teach: *nightmare, snoring, recurring dream*. Write the following questions on the board for discussion in pairs (5 mins): *How often do you dream? Do you often have nightmares or recurring dreams? Do you think that dreams have any meaning?*

2 Letters to Dreamtime

Divide the class into three or four groups and hand out the same text to the students in each group. Tell them that they are going to read a letter that has been sent in to a professional dream psychoanalyst. Explain psychoanalyst to the students (A professional trained in analysing the mind). Give them six to eight minutes to read their letter and the reply. They can also do the vocabulary check, matching the words up to their definitions. Monitor to check correct answers.

Answers
Text A 1c 2h 3f 4a 5g 6b 7d 8e
Text B 1c 2e 3a 4g 5b 6h 7f 8d (7&8 v. similar)
Text C 1d 2f 3a 4b 5g 6h 7e 8c
Text D 1c 2d 3f 4e 5a 6b

When they have finished, ask them to discuss the following questions for five minutes: *What was the dream about? What does it mean? Have you ever had a similar dream?*

3 Psychoanalysis

Re-group the students so that in each new group there are four (or three) students who have each read different letters. The students should take it in turns to read out their letter to Dreamtime (not the reply). The other students now try to interpret the dream, playing the role of the Dreamtime psychoanalyst and saying what they think it means. When they have finished, the first student can read out the reply from Dreamtime, saying whose interpretation was most accurate. They should continue around the group in this way until they have all read out their letters.

Tip: Encourage the students to make notes while listening to each other's letters. This will help them to provide more detailed interpretations.

4 Class feedback

Find out who, in each group, interpreted the dreams most accurately, and who made the most creative interpretations.

5 Personalisation

Now tell the students that they are going to share their own dreams with each other. Keep them in the same groups.

Tip: Try putting on some relaxing music.

Tell them to spend five minutes making brief notes about their own dreams, including recent dreams, childhood dreams and nightmares. Then tell them to talk about their dreams, offering each other interpretations of each dream based on what they have learnt in the lesson.

Extension: Dream Facts

Hand out the Dream Facts questionnaire (one per group of three or four) and set a time limit (5 mins). When they have finished, check the answers, getting one or two predictions for each before you reveal the correct answer.

Answers
1 True **2** False. In fact we dream one or two hours every night on average. The second part is true. **3** True. Blind people do dream. Although their dreams may not consist of visual images, blind people can clearly remember the sounds they hear or the textures they come into contact with in their dreams. **4** False. **5** False. In fact, five minutes after the end of the dream, half the content is forgotten. After ten minutes, 90% is lost. **6** True **7** True **8** True. According to the experts. **9** False **10** False. I just made it up!

Text A

Dreams Can Come True

Rotting Teeth

Dear Dreamtime,

I had a dream that I bit on something that was hard and a tooth fell out. Quickly all of my teeth started rotting and falling out. I pulled back my cheek with my hand to look at my back teeth and half of my lower jaw fell out into my hand. I was terrified! I put it back into place before anyone saw it and ran to my boyfriend for comfort to tell him what was happening. I said, "Look at my teeth!" and he said, angrily, "What are you doing?" That was the end of the dream.

Anne C.

Dear Anne,

Dreams about losing your teeth typically represents your worries about your appearance and how you think others see you. You may be feeling unattractive and this may be reflected in your dream.

Nonetheless, it is important to explore the relationship you have with your boyfriend. You mentioned how you ran to him for comfort, but instead of helping, he sounded like he was more or less blaming you for the situation. He said "What are you doing?" as if it was your fault that your teeth fell out and that you had done something to make them fall out. This may reflect a deeper problem between you and your boyfriend. Perhaps he has blamed you for something that was beyond your control? Or maybe he is making little jokes about your physical appearance and in your mind you feel he would like you to look a certain way and that you are not meeting his expectations of beauty. Or you might even be putting pressure on yourself, worried about what he is thinking.

Best regards,
Dreamtime

Read the letter to Dreamtime, and the answer. Complete the vocabulary check as you read by matching each word to its meaning:

Vocabulary check

1 *rotting*
2 *cheek*
3 *jaw*
4 *reflect*
5 *nonetheless*
6 *explore*
7 *blame (blaming)*
8 *expectations*

a) show an image of something (e.g. in a mirror or in water)
b) (*here*) examine, or look at something in detail
c) going bad (e.g. fruit or meat)
d) tell someone that they caused a problem, that it's their fault
e) the things you think or hope will happen in the future
f) the bottom part of your skull (*see picture*)
g) but / anyway (often used to start a new idea)
h) part of your face between your ear and your mouth

Text B

Dreams Can Come True

Flimsy Nightgown

Dear Dreamtime,

Over the last few months I've had a recurring dream. I'm sitting on the bus on the way to work and I realise I'm in my flimsy nightgown. What am I going to do? I end up getting off the bus in the centre of town and walking towards the building where I work, trying to ignore people staring at me. It's a very uncomfortable feeling. Yet I always seem to wake up before I get to the office.

Carla J.

Hi Carla,

Your dream suggests that you are torn between two different roles in your life. There is a conflict between how you feel and the role you are playing. Your flimsy nightgown probably makes you feel exposed, suggesting that some aspect of your life is making you vulnerable. The fact that you are on your way to work, also suggests that your vulnerability might relate to your work. Next time you have the same dream, look carefully among the crowds. You may notice someone from work or an acquaintance. Often this may be a manager or superior who is putting pressure on you to do better. Perhaps you feel inadequate in your performance at work?

Best regards,
Dreamtime

Read the letter to Dreamtime, and the answer. Complete the vocabulary check as you read by matching each word to its meaning:

Vocabulary check

1 *flimsy*
2 *recurring*
3 *ignore*
4 *staring*
5 *be torn between*
6 *conflict (n)*
7 *exposed*
8 *vulnerable*

a) not pay attention to someone or something on purpose
b) be trying to make a difficult decision (usually with just two options)
c) (*here*) thin and see-through
d) open to danger, unable to protect yourself
e) repeating
f) unprotected from something (e.g. the weather or danger)
g) looking at something intensively
h) fight, argument, war

Text C

Dreams Can Come True

Chased By A Spider

Dear Dreamtime,

I had a dream where I woke up in the middle of the night and then walked up to my attic. There was a huge spider's web being spun by a giant spider. It chased me into a corner. I jumped out of the nearest window onto the street but it continued to chase me through the streets of central London (At some points I was jumping across the tops of cars to get away from it). I woke up before it caught me.

James V.

Dear James,

Your dream suggests that you are feeling trapped in a present situation or relationship. Do you feel that somebody is taking advantage of you? You really want to get out of this situation, but you are afraid to confront it. As with many chase dreams, fear and anxiety are the main reasons why you are running away. When you dream that you wake up, it means that you have made some new discovery.

It's not surprising that your dream leads you to the attic. Being located upstairs, the attic is often the symbol of your mind and thoughts. So this relationship with the spider is probably occupying your mind. Is there one thing that you have been thinking about and you can't get it out of your mind? Most importantly, ask yourself who or what is the spider!

Best regards,
Dreamtime

Read the letter to Dreamtime, and the answer. Complete the vocabulary check as you read by matching each word to its meaning:

Vocabulary check

1 *chase*
2 *attic*
3 *web*
4 *spun*
5 *trapped*
6 *confront*
7 *anxiety*
8 *occupying*

a) a net made by a spider (*see picture*)
b) (from spin) make a web
c) taking up space or time
d) run after someone / something to catch it
e) worry caused by problems or fears
f) the room at the top of many houses (for storage)
g) stuck / unable to escape
h) recognise and deal with (especially a problem)

Dreams Can Come True

Flying Out of Control

Dear Dreamtime,

I am 29 years old and for many years I have had a recurring dream. When I was a teenager I would dream that I was flying over the earth with a long rope tied to my waist. Sometimes, the rope broke and I started flying out into space. I got scared, grabbed the rope and pulled myself back down to earth.

More recently, I find myself running in my dreams and when I jump I start flying up into the air. Then I start falling back down to the earth. This happens a couple of times until I get scared because I know it will really hurt when I hit the ground. I wake myself up and I am almost in tears. Why is this happening to me and what does this mean? Please help me understand. Is this some sort of a sign?

Julie R.

Hi Julie,

Your childhood dreams of flying seem to suggest fears of letting go and exploring the world on your own. This may come from a sheltered upbringing.

Jumping in dreams represents risks and challenges. Is there a new situation in your life making you feel both excited and anxious? Perhaps you are not sure how to approach this challenge. It seems that you are uncomfortable with being in the air (as you were when you were younger). This may be to do with a fear of failure. Sometimes you need to break free and take a chance. Even if you don't land on your feet, you need to get up and try again.

Best regards,
Dreamtime

Read the letter to Dreamtime, and the answer. Complete the vocabulary check as you read by matching each word to its meaning:

Vocabulary check

1 *recurring*
2 *rope*
3 *sheltered upbringing*
4 *challenge*
5 *anxious*
6 *failure*

a) feeling worried about a problem or fear
b) opposite of success
c) repeating
d) strong material often used for climbing (*see picture*)
e) a difficult, but important test
f) a childhood with very protective parents

Dreams Can Come True

Dream Facts

Here are ten interesting facts about dreams. Five are true and five are false, but which are which? Put a ✔ by the ones you think are true, and a ✗ by the ones you think are false.

1 The Romans submitted unusual dreams to the Senate (parliament) for analysis and interpretation.

2 We dream, on average, for three or four hours every night. And we often have four to seven dreams in one night.

3 Blind people have dreams like the rest of us, only without images.

4 If you die in your dream, you actually die in real life.

5 Twelve minutes after the end of a dream, half the content is forgotten. After 20 minutes, 80% is lost.

6 Men tend to dream more about other men, while women dream equally about men and women.

7 Young children do not dream about themselves. They do not appear in their own dreams until the age of three or four.

8 If you are snoring, then you cannot be dreaming.

9 If you leave the light on, you are more likely to have a nightmare.

10 The Aztecs of Central America believed that their dreams were the 'real' world, and that their waking world was just a personal fantasy.

Dreams Can Come True

Dream Facts

Here are ten interesting facts about dreams. Five are true and five are false, but which are which? Put a ✔ by the ones you think are true, and a ✗ by the ones you think are false.

1 The Romans submitted unusual dreams to the Senate (parliament) for analysis and interpretation.

2 We dream, on average, for three or four hours every night. And we often have four to seven dreams in one night.

3 Blind people have dreams like the rest of us, only without images.

4 If you die in your dream, you actually die in real life.

5 Twelve minutes after the end of a dream, half the content is forgotten. After 20 minutes, 80% is lost.

6 Men tend to dream more about other men, while women dream equally about men and women.

7 Young children do not dream about themselves. They do not appear in their own dreams until the age of three or four.

8 If you are snoring, then you cannot be dreaming.

9 If you leave the light on, you are more likely to have a nightmare.

10 The Aztecs of Central America believed that their dreams were the 'real' world, and that their waking world was just a personal fantasy.

2 First Time Buyers: Teacher's notes

Topic focus	Houses and homes; Furniture; Interior design
Grammar / Functional focus	Negotiating prices; *There is / are* for description; *Have to / need* for expressing necessity
Level / Number of students	Intermediate – Advanced / Minimum six students
Time	35–45 minutes (Extension 15 minutes)

Preparation

For each group of six to twelve students make one copy of all the property sheets and one copy per student of either the estate agent or the buyer role card (see below).

Tip: Preparation for a role play is important. If students understand the role and prepare well, they will usually perform much better. Encourage them to invent colourful characters!

1 Suggested lead-in

Pre-teach *estate agent* and write the following questions on the board for discussion in pairs (5 mins): *What is an estate agent? What do they do? What kind of qualities do you need to be an estate agent? What are the advantages and disadvantages of the job?*

2 The role cards

Divide the class up into estate agents and buyers. There should be three to four estate agents per group. Give each estate agent in the group a different property information card. There should be three to eight buyers per group (they can work alone or in pairs, depending on group numbers). For larger classes, create two or more groups. Give each of the estate agents and buyers a copy of their role card. Let them read their cards. Give the buyers three minutes to think up characters for themselves. Meanwhile, the estate agents should think up questions to ask the buyers.

3 The role play

The buyers 'enter the shop' and are greeted by one of the estate agents. After about two to three minutes, rotate the pairings so that after eight to ten minutes all the buyers have 'viewed' all the properties. Give them five more minutes to make their choice and close a sale!

4 Round up

Get some feedback. Ask the estate agents what prices they got for their properties and ask the buyers whether they are happy with their new flat.

Extension – Furnishing the flat

Tell the students that they are going to furnish a new flat they have recently bought. Hand out the floor plan (*below*), one copy to each pair. Tell them to decide which rooms to use as bedrooms, living room etc. then to agree on the furniture for each room, drawing it on the floor plan as they decide. When they have finished, re-pair them to compare their solutions and explain their choices.

First Time Buyers: Furnishing the Flat

Congratulations! This is your new two-bedroom flat. You must decide which room will be the lounge, kitchen, etc. and then add all the furniture. Draw the chairs, cupboards, tables, beds, etc. Remember, there are two of you!

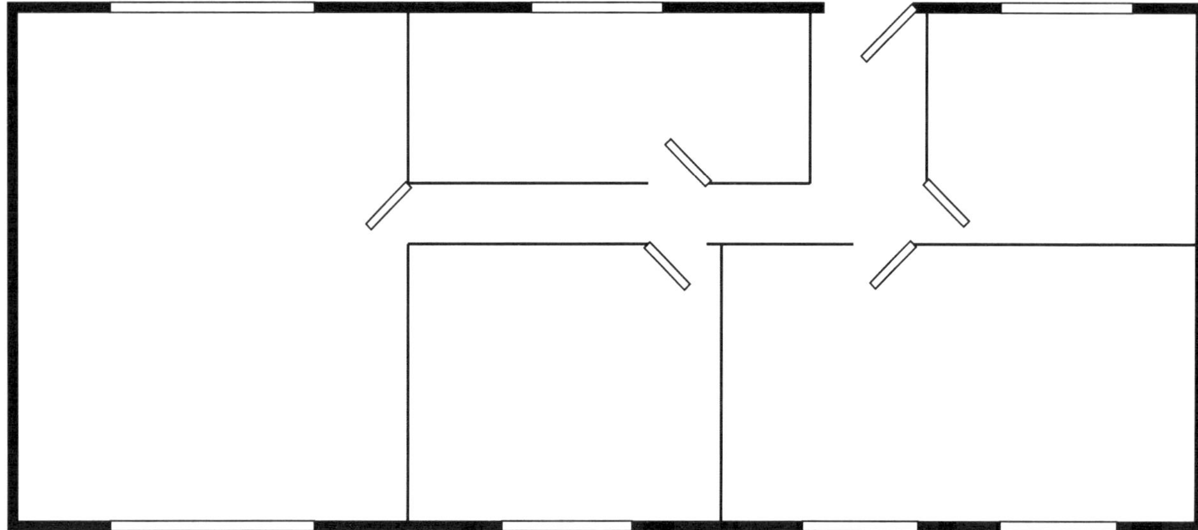

First Time Buyers

A 32 Craymore Terrace, London W2

£369,000

A two-bedroom, two-bathroom flat on the first floor of a period building with an attractive, large balcony and beautiful views of a delightful neighbourhood. Private parking space and private security guard. Feel safe in the heart of London. This flat is perfect for anyone who loves to impress!

Reception Room 5m x 4.5m
A bright room with a high ceiling and doors to front-facing balcony. Original fireplace.

Open Plan Kitchen
Impressive fitted units make the most of space, with built-in oven. Sink, fitted washing machine and dishwasher.

Bedroom One 3.2m x 2.8m
Windows to rear, built-in cupboard and door leading to en suite bathroom.

En Suite Bathroom
Spacious and full of light. Bath, WC and washbasin.

Bedroom Two 1.8m x 1.7m
Windows to front, balcony access, private shower room.

Shower Room
Newly-fitted shower, sink and WC.

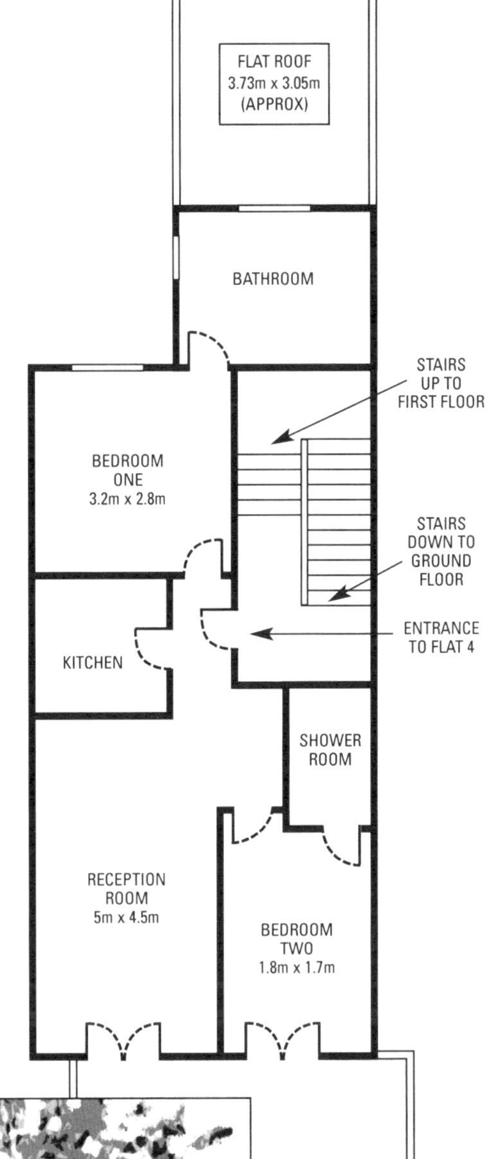

First Time Buyers

B 46a Hangar Drive, London W3

£349,000

A two-bedroom, one-bathroom flat with separate WC, fully modernised, on the ground floor of a period property. Doors in reception room lead to a pretty, private garden with lots of potential. High ceilings and original doors give the property plenty of character.

Reception Room 4.8m x 4m
Window and door to rear, wooden floors, original fireplace, built-in shelves with spotlights.

Kitchen 3.2m x 2m
Beautiful wooden wall units with modern worktops. Stainless steel sink and oven with extractor above, integrated washing machine, fridge/freezer, dishwasher and tiled floor. Recently fitted.

Bedroom One 4.9m x 3.1m
Large window to front, wooden floors, original fireplace, fitted cupboards and wardrobe.

Bathroom
Window above door. New WC, bath with stainless steel shower and glass screen, two sinks, tiled walls and floor, spotlights.

Bedroom Two 4.7m x 2m
Window to front, wooden floors, spotlights and radiator.

Separate WC
Window to rear, sink and WC. Storage cupboards above.

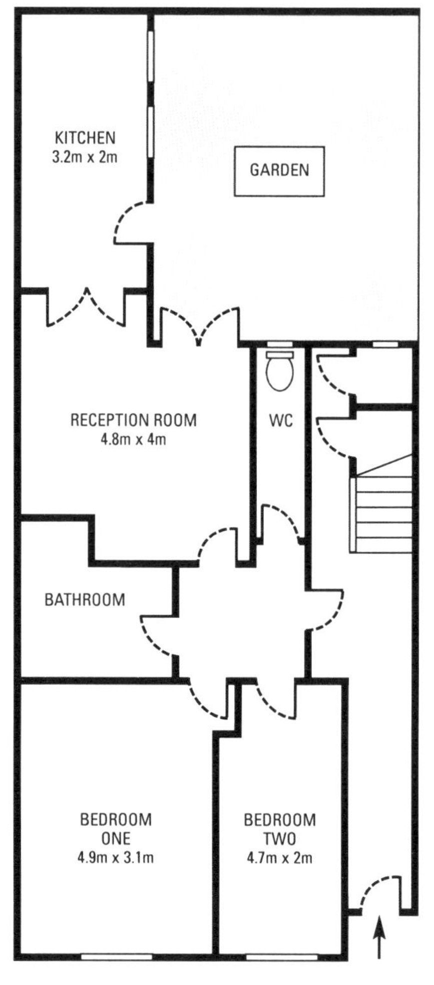

First Time Buyers

130 Fountain Gardens, London W4

£385,000

A well-designed, two-bedroom, two-bathroom apartment on the top floor of a 16-storey modern block. Large reception room and balcony with spectacular views. This apartment has a real feel of luxury about it and has been kept in very good condition.

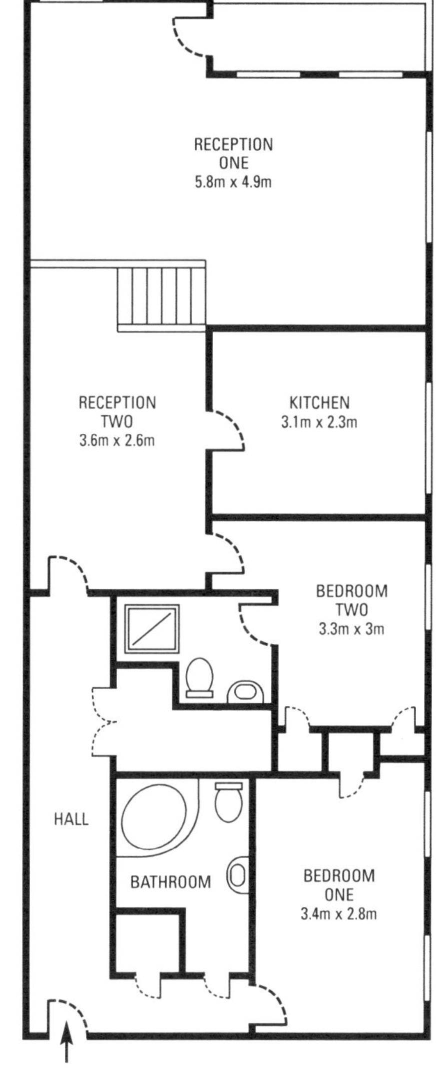

Hallway
Storage cupboards, radiators and spotlights.

Bathroom
Stylish corner bath, WC, built-in wash basin, tiled walls and floor, spotlights.

Bedroom One 3.4m x 2.8m
Two windows with spectacular views over London, radiator and fitted cupboard.

Bedroom Two 3.3m x 3m
Window with views over Paddington, radiator, two fitted cupboards and door to:

En Suite Shower Room
Hand basin, shower cubicle and tiled walls and floor.

Reception Two 3.6m x 2.6m
Balcony rail, dining area and doors to:

Kitchen 3.1m x 2.3m
Window with spectacular views, wall units with worktops, white sink, large, modern electric oven, dishwasher, fridge freezer, built-in washing machine, tiled walls.

Stairs down from Reception Two, to:

Reception One 5.8m x 4.9m
Windows to side and front, door to balcony offering amazing panoramic views across London, two radiators.

First Time Buyers

D 6b Ashley Way, London NW2

£359,000

A two-bedroom, two-bathroom flat on the top floor of this three-storey building, with the added benefits of a terrace and parking for residents.

Entrance Hall
Entry phone system, storage cupboards and doors to:

Bedroom One 3.8m x 3.5m
Spacious bedroom with window to rear, radiator and door to:

En Suite Bathroom
Bath, shower and hand basin, window to rear. Storage cupboard.

Bathroom
To be newly fitted with bath, shower, WC and hand basin.

Kitchen 4m x 2.1m
Window to rear, fitted wall units, sink, washing-machine and oven.

Reception Room 5.2m x 3.4m
Windows to front and back, doors to terrace, pleasant views of garden and tree-lined street. Single radiator and spotlighting.

Bedroom Two 3.6m x 2.4m
Bow window to front, single radiator.

Role Cards

First Time Buyers

Estate agent

The teacher will give you the information card to a two-bedroom flat in central London. You have to sell the flat to one of the buyers (other students) in the office today. Try to get as much as you can for it (up to £400,000), but don't sell it for less than £300,000. Don't close the deal until you have talked to all the customers! Good luck.

Before you begin, check the **key vocabulary** and **useful expressions** below and write a few more questions to ask the customers.

Key vocabulary

fitted (cupboard, units, etc.) – fixed to the walls, part of the flat
newly fitted / recently fitted – new
period property – over 100 years old, with typical architecture for the period
bow window – a cylinder shaped (round) window
three-storey – three floors
spacious – big, with lots of space inside
storage (cupboard, space) – wardrobes or cupboards for putting things in
spotlighting / spotlights – small lights built into the ceiling
WC – toilet
reception (room) – living room / lounge

Useful expressions

Can I interest you in...
All the rooms have...
...in an excellent location
...in excellent condition
...with incredible views...
...great value for money
...other buyers have shown some interest...
I can't negotiate on the price...

Questions to ask the customers

How much do you want to spend?
____________________?
____________________?

Have you got any children?
____________________?
____________________?

First Time Buyers

Buyers

You are looking for a two-bedroom flat in central London. You have a maximum of £400,000 to spend, but ideally you don't want to go over £350,000. You are going to visit some estate agents. Talk to all the agents, explain exactly what you want and then listen to what they've got. Take your time to choose the best flat and try to get the best price!

Before you begin, decide on the following:

1 Are you single or married?
2 Do you have children?
3 What job do you do?
4 Do you want a garden or a beautiful view?

Think of some more special requests. You can decide who you are in a role play!

Key vocabulary

fitted (cupboard, units, etc.) – fixed to the walls, part of the flat
newly fitted / recently fitted – new
period property – over 100 years old, with typical architecture for the period
bow window – a cylinder shaped (round) window
three-storey – three floors
spacious – big, with lots of space inside
storage (cupboard, space) – wardrobes or cupboards for putting things in
spotlighting / spotlights – small lights built into the ceiling
WC – toilet
reception (room) – living room / lounge

Useful expressions

I'm / We're interested in...
The flat has to have...
I can't stand (busy streets).
I'm looking for something more...
...would be very useful.
We need...
That price is far too high.
Can we negotiate?
My maximum offer is...

3 Aesop's Fables: Teacher's notes

Topic focus Animals; Making mistakes; Parts of the body

Grammar / Functional focus Time expressions; Reported speech; Past simple and narrative tenses

Level / Number of students Intermediate to Upper intermediate / Minimum four students

Time 40–50 minutes (Extension 20–30 minutes)

Preparation

Copy and cut up the first two stories (one of either story per student), the third story and 'Fable Farm' (one of both per group of two to four students). Also make two to three copies of the six stories at the end. Cut up all the sheets as indicated.

1 Suggested lead-in

Draw pictures of a hare and a tortoise on the board. Elicit the story and ask: What's the moral of the story? (*Slowly but surely wins the race.*) Ask the students: *Who wrote the story?* (Aesop) and find out what they know about him (see *Notes on Aesop* below).

2 Jigsaw reading

Divide the class into two groups, A and B. Give *The Fox and the Stork* to the students in group A and *The Lion and the Mouse* to group B. Tell them to read the story and put the words of the moral in the correct order. As they finish, they can do the vocabulary check.

Answers
The Fox and the Stork 1c 2g 3e 4a 5h 6b 7f 8d
Moral: You always get what you deserve (explain *deserve*)
The Lion and the Mouse 1c 2g 3a 4f 5b 6d 7h 8e
Moral: Little friends might one day be great friends

3 Jigsaw exchange

Now re-pair one group A student with one group B student and ask them to retell their story in their own words.

Tip: *Encourage the students to use their own words as much as possible, only referring to the text when they can't remember what happens next or when they need a specific word or expression.*

Monitor and prompt the students if necessary. If you've studied reported speech recently, tell them to use it where possible.

4 The Fox and the Goat (optional)

Hand out a copy of the story *The Fox and the Goat* to each pair. Give them five minutes to read the story and complete the gaps with their own ideas. Tell them that there is no right answer, and that the choice is theirs. When they finish, get one or two suggestions for each gap. Possible answers are given below.

Answers
1 What are you doing down there? **2** have lots of water **3** looked up at the sky **4** to the river **5** It is starting right now **6** jumped into the well **7** jumped out of the well **8** Goodbye, fool! Enjoy the drought!
Moral: Look before you leap (or: Never trust the advice of a man in trouble)
Vocabulary check: 1d 2f 3b 4a 5c 6e

Now give them five minutes to go through the discussion questions. Monitor.

Answers
1 Fox is usually the bad guy, crafty and untrustworthy. He usually loses out, but not always! **2** Stork is usually wise and careful. Goat is usually stupid and gullible. Lion is always strong and noble – king. Mouse varies, but is often hard-working and quick-thinking. **3** Fox tried to play practical joke on stork, but it backfired. Goat believed advice of desperate fox. Lion was careless when walking in forest. He also thought only powerful friends are important. Questions 4–7 require personal answers: elicit from students.

Extension: Fable Farm

Put students into groups of three or four and hand out the Fable Farm worksheet, one per group. Read the instructions and check they understand the meaning of all five morals. Remind them that this is not a writing exercise. They should create a fable (traditionally spoken stories). One secretary in each group can make notes. After 15–20 minutes tell each group to choose one student to tell their story to the class. When they have finished, give out copies of the original stories. Often the storylines are similar.

Suggestion: *Students could write up their fable for homework.*

Notes on Aesop
Aesop was probably born in 620 BC in Greece. He was born a slave, but he earned his freedom from his second master due to his learning and wit. He quickly rose to political prominence and took on an ambassadorial role for King Croesus, using his fables to instruct the people of Greece how to act wisely. He was executed by the people of Delphi after he refused to pass on some money to them from Croesus, fearing they would misuse it. Soon after that several calamities befell the citizens of Delphi. The expression 'The blood of Aesop' derives from this event.

Aesop's Fables

Read the story and then put the words of the moral in the right order.

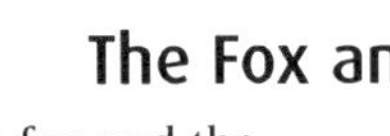

The Fox and the Stork

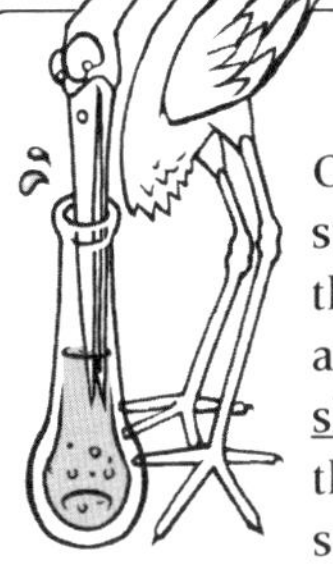

Once, many years ago, the fox and the stork were very good friends. So one day the fox invited the stork to dinner, and, for a joke, he gave her some soup in a very <u>shallow</u> <u>bowl</u>. The fox could easily drink the soup from the shallow bowl, but the stork couldn't. She could only get the end of her long <u>beak</u> wet! When the meal was finished, she was much hungrier than before it began.

"I am sorry," said the fox, "that you don't like soup. As for me – it's my favourite dish!"

"Please do not <u>apologise</u>," said the stork. "I hope you will come and have dinner with me soon."

"With pleasure!" said the fox, and <u>licked</u> his greedy lips.

So they agreed, and the next week the fox came to the stork's house for dinner. When he sat down at the table, he was very surprised to see a long <u>jar</u> with a very <u>narrow</u> neck in front of him. And inside was soup, the fox's favourite food! The stork began drinking, but the fox just sat there watching <u>helplessly</u>! The jar was too narrow for him to drink the soup. The best he could do was to lick the sides. After she had finished eating, the stork said:

"I am sorry, that you don't like soup. I thought you said it was your favourite dish!"

deserve • get • what • you • always • you

Vocabulary check

1 *shallow*	a) say sorry
2 *bowl*	b) a container for water, etc.
3 *beak*	c) opposite of *deep*
4 *apologise*	d) unable to improve the situation
5 *licked*	e) a bird's mouth
6 *jar*	f) opposite of *wide*
7 *narrow*	g) a container for soup or cereal
8 *helplessly*	h) tasted with his tongue

Aesop's Fables

Read the story and then put the words of the moral in the right order.

The Lion and the Mouse

One day the lion was lying, sleeping in the afternoon sun. A tiny mouse came up to him and began running up and down the back of the great lion. The lion soon woke up, and caught the little mouse in his <u>paw</u>. He was angry that his sleep had been <u>disturbed</u> but the mouse was an easy meal, so he opened his mouth to <u>swallow</u> him.

"Pardon me, King Lion," said the mouse in a high voice. "I didn't mean to wake you up. Please forgive me and one day I might be able to do you a favour."

The lion laughed at the idea that this tiny animal might be able to help him.

"You have a lot of <u>courage</u> for one so small," he said and let the mouse go.

A few years later the lion was walking through the forest when he got caught in a <u>hunter</u>'s <u>snare</u>.

"Oh no!" he <u>roared</u>. "When the hunters return they will surely kill me!"

Just then, the little mouse came along and remembered the lion from a few years ago.

"Pardon me, King Lion," he said in a high voice, "perhaps I can help you."

With these words, the tiny mouse ran up to the snare and began <u>chewing</u> through the snare with his sharp teeth.

"Was I not right?" said the mouse, and they walked off together, friends forever.

friends • day • great • might • one • be • friends • little

Vocabulary check

1 *paw*	a) pass food or drink from the mouth to the stomach
2 *disturbed*	b) someone who catches animals for food
3 *swallow*	c) an animal's foot
4 *courage*	d) a trap for catching animals
5 *hunter*	e) breaking up food with your teeth
6 *snare (n)*	f) if you have this, you are not scared of danger
7 *roared*	g) interrupted
8 *chewing*	h) called loudly (like a lion)

Aesop's Fables

Here is another fable by Aesop. Read through and complete the gaps with your own ideas.

The Fox and the Goat

One day, by bad luck, the fox fell into a deep well, from which he could not get out. Soon after the goat came along and saw the fox in the well.

"________________________________?" the goat asked.

"Haven't you heard?" said the fox, "There's going to be a great drought soon, so I jumped down here to ________________________________ during the difficult times ahead. Why don't you come and join me?"

The goat felt worried by what the fox said, so she ________________________________. It was blue, with no clouds about. She went ________________________________ and saw that there wasn't much water there, either. She went back to the well. "When is the drought starting?" she asked the fox.

"________________________________!" the fox said, "Be quick and jump in beside me. There is only enough room for two in this small well."

The goat thought this was the best idea and ________________________________. But as soon as she did, the fox immediately jumped up on her back, put his paws on her long horns and ________________________________.

"________________________________!" said the fox as he ran off.

Now think of your own moral for this fable:

Vocabulary check

1 *well* — d) a hole in the ground for getting water
2 *drought*
3 *clouds*
4 *beside*
5 *paws*
6 *horns*

a) next to
b) white things in the sky; they make rain
c) an animal's feet
d) a hole in the ground for getting water
e) goats have two of them on their head
f) a long time without rain

Discussion

1 In Aesop's stories, what role does the fox usually play?
2 What about the other animals? Which is stupid / clever, hard-working, etc?
3 What mistakes did the fox, the goat and the lion make?
4 Have you ever made any similar mistakes in your life?
5 Which story do you like best? Why?
6 Which story do you think has the most important moral?
7 Do you think these stories are good for teaching children about the real world? Why (not)?

Fable Farm

Work in groups of three to four students. Look at these five morals. All of them have been taken from fables by Aesop.

1 You should always prepare for difficult times in the future.
2 A fool is always a fool, even in fine clothes.
3 Never pretend to be something that you are not.
4 Even the wise are foolish when they fall in love.
5 It is better to starve and be free than to be a fat slave.

Choose one of them and think of a fable to illustrate it. Think about these things:

- Which animals are most suitable to the story?
- How and where did the animals meet?
- What happened between them?
- How did the story end?

Don't write your fable out in full, but it's a good idea if one member of the group takes notes. Prepare it well and choose one member of your group to tell the fable to the rest of the class after you have finished.

When you've finished, you can compare your story with the original by Aesop.

How different were they? Which do you prefer? Why?

Aesop's Fables

1 The Ant and the Grasshopper

In a field one summer's day a grasshopper was hopping about, singing happily and playing. An ant passed by, carrying a heavy leaf he was taking to the nest.

"Why not come and chat with me," said the grasshopper, "instead of working so hard on a lovely day?"

"I am helping to collect food for the winter," said the ant, "and I recommend you do the same."

"Why worry about winter?" said the grasshopper, "We have got lots of food at the moment." But the ant didn't listen to him and went on his way.

Several months later, when the winter came, the grasshopper had no food and began to die of hunger. Not far away, he saw the ants working hard, but they were healthy, thanks to the food they had collected in the summer. Then the grasshopper knew:

You should always prepare for difficult times in the future.

2 The Ass in the Lion's Skin

One day an ass found a lion's skin which had been left by the hunters in the forest to dry in the sun. The ass liked the skin, and thought he would look nice in it, so he put it on. He went to the lake and saw how beautiful he looked, so he decided to keep it on.

He went back to his village wearing the skin. Everybody panicked, because they thought he was a lion. He thought this was very funny and began to laugh like an ass. Suddenly everyone recognised his voice, and they were very angry with him. His owner beat him, and he was very sorry for what he had done.

A fool is always a fool, even in fine clothes.

3 The Monkey and the Dolphin

A monkey, who lived on a ship, always dreamed he could visit the ports that the ship went into.

"It must be so fantastic," he said to the rats on the ship, "to visit these places. I wish I was a human."

Then one day there was a strong storm, and the ship sank into the sea. A dolphin saw the monkey swimming for his life and thought he was a man and needed help. So he rescued the monkey and took him to the nearest city, which was Athens.

Just as they were coming towards Athens, the dolphin asked the monkey: "Are you from Athens?"

"Yes," said the monkey, "And I am from one of the richest families in the city."

"Really?," said the dolphin, "So you must know Piraeus, then."

The dolphin was talking about the famous port of Athens, but the monkey thought he was talking about a famous man.

"Yes, he is one of my best friends." he said.

The dolphin suddenly realised his mistake and looked up to see that his passenger was really a monkey, not a human. He swam down under the water and drowned the monkey.

Never pretend to be something that you are not.

4 The Lion in Love

A lion fell in love with a beautiful girl who lived in the village. He demanded her hand in marriage from her father, a woodcutter. The father didn't want his daughter to marry a lion, but he was too frightened to say no, so he said to the lion, "She can marry you, but only if you let me take out your big teeth and claws, because she is very frightened that they might hurt her."

"Very well," said the lion, without thinking, and the woodcutter took them out.

"Now, when shall we arrange the wedding?" asked the lion.

The woodcutter laughed and picked up his biggest axe. "What wedding?" he said, and chased the lion out of the village!

Even the wise are foolish when they fall in love.

5 The Dog and the Wolf

A thin wolf, almost dead with hunger, was walking in the forest one day when he met a house dog who was alone.

"Ah, cousin," said the dog, "you look terrible. Your hard way of life will soon kill you. Why don't you do as I do and work steadily for a master? That way, your food is guaranteed, every day in a bowl."

"I would like that," said the wolf, "but how can I get a place?"

"I can arrange that for you," said the dog. "Come with me to my master and you can share my work."

So the wolf and the dog set off together for the village. Along the way, the wolf noticed that the dog had very thin hair around his neck, and he asked the dog how this had happened.

"Oh, that's nothing," said the dog. "It's just the mark left by the collar I have to wear each night so that they can chain me up. It hurts a bit, but you soon get used to it."

"A chain?" asked the wolf, very surprised. "Then goodbye to you, cousin. I will be spending this night starving in the woods."

It is better to starve and be free than to be a fat slave.

4 In Actual Fact: Teacher's notes

Topic focus	News / newspapers; The law; Crime; The family
Grammar / Functional focus	Forming / asking questions; Phrasal verbs
Level / Number of students	Intermediate to Upper intermediate / Minimum three students
Time	30–40 minutes (Extension 10 minutes)

Preparation

Copy all three texts (one of either A, B or C per student). Also make one copy of the Censored task (*below*) per group of three students. You could also keep the key questions and answers (*below*) for the students to check in stage 4.

1 Suggested lead-in

Pre-teach: *adopt, prison, trial, legal action, sentenced (to...)* Write the following questions on the board for discussion in pairs (5 mins): *Do you believe everything you read in the papers? Why (not)? How often do you think newspapers make mistakes / get facts wrong?*

Suggestion: *If your students would find it interesting, write two or three current news headlines on the board. Elicit the basic details from the students and discuss them for a few minutes.*

2 Read the article

Divide the class into three groups of equal numbers. Give out the same text to the students in each group. Students read the text (4–6 minutes). Monitor carefully. Difficult words are underlined and explained in the vocabulary check.

3 Find the differences

Re-group the students so that in each new group there is at least one student who has read each of the three texts. Read the Key Task. With weak intermediate groups, write the first word of each question on the board: 1. When...? 2. Why...? etc. (*see below*) Monitor carefully. They should correct the mistakes as they find them.

4 Class feedback

When all the groups have finished, check the answers by asking the key questions (*above right*). The correct answers are given. The letters in brackets indicate which two of the three texts have each fact correct.

Key Questions and Answers (correct texts)
1 When did Brian and Julie adopt Mark? 1979. (B&C) **2** Why did Donna give up Mark? Her father advised her to do it. (A&B) **3** What didn't Andrew know? About the adoption. (A&C) **4** Why did Andrew begin legal action? He wanted to bring up Mark himself. (A&B) **5** Where did Brian and Julie take Mark? New Mexico. (B&C) **6** What did they change their names to? Barney and Helen Powers. (A&C) **7** How long did they live there? For over 20 years. (A&C) **8** How did the police discover that the name was false? After Mark applied to be a police officer. (A&B) **9** How long did the trial take? Almost a year. (A&C) **10** How much did Brian and Julie have to pay to Andrew? $100,000. (B&C) **11** Why did they have to pay so much? Because Mr Rocco had spent the money looking for his son. (A&B) **12** How long was Brian sent to prison for? Two years. (A&B) **13** What was he sentenced for? Kidnapping. (B&C) **14** How long was Julie sentenced for? Six months. (A&C) **15** What did Mark say after the trial? (see texts) (B&C)

5 Discussion

Students discuss the questions at the bottom of their sheet (5-10 mins). This is a true story from August 2002, only the names and the pictures have been changed. In answer to the second question, the true son was extremely angry with his birth father for bringing charges against his 'adopted' parents, to whom he remained loyal.

Extension: Censored

If you have time, do this activity after the discussion. Tell the students to hide their original texts and then give out the 'Censored' text (*below*). Working together as a group of three, they should recall the story (no writing), thinking up an appropriate phrase for each gap. Although they may not remember all the details, they should still be able to think up a suitable alternative.

In Actual Fact... Censored!

Re-tell the story, trying to remember the details that have been removed.

■■■ Brian and Julie Taylor ■■■ New York ■■■ and ■■■ him Mark. Mark's birth ■■■, Donna McGee ■■■ the child on the ■■■. Unfortunately, Mark's birth father, Andrew Rocco, ■■■ know ■■■. He wasn't married ■■■ Donna ■■■. Mr Rocco wanted to ■■■ up the baby himself, ■■■ legal ■■■ to get his son ■■■. Brian and Julie ■■■ Mark and were ■■■ about ■■■. So they ■■■ away with their baby ■■■. They changed their ■■■ to Barney and Helen Powers. For ■■■ 20 years ■■■ New Mexico, a happy, friendly ■■■ with ■■■. Then in

2001, ■■■ a police ■■■ and the police discovered that ■■■. Brian (or Barney) decided ■■■ to the police. The trial ■■■ ■■■. Brian and Julie ■■■ $100,000 to Mr Rocco, who had ■■■ the money ■■■ his ■■■ son. Brian Taylor ■■■ two years in ■■■ for kidnapping and his ■■■ six ■■■. After the trial Mark said ■■■ Mr and Mrs Taylor: "■■■ people I love very ■■■. Now ■■■ ■■■ it's ■■■ over."

In Actual Fact

Text A

THE NEW YORK OBSERVER

In 1977 Brian and Julie Taylor from New York adopted a son and called him Mark. Mark's birth mother, Donna McGee, gave up the child on the advice of her father. Unfortunately, Mark's birth father, Andrew Rocco, didn't know about the adoption. He wasn't married to Donna at the time. Mr Rocco wanted to bring up the baby himself, so he began legal action to get his son back. Brian and Julie already loved Mark and were worried about losing him. So they ran away with their baby to New Jersey. They changed their names to Barney and Helen Powers. For over 20 years they lived in New Jersey, a happy, friendly family with a big secret. Then in 2001, Mark applied to be a police officer and the police discovered that their name was false. Brian decided to give himself up to the police. The trial took almost a year. Brian and Julie were told to pay $10,000 to Mr Rocco, who had spent the money looking for his lost son. Brian Taylor was sentenced to two years in prison for deception and his wife Julie received six months.

After the trial Mark said about Mr and Mrs Taylor, "These are two people I hate so much! Now I'm just glad that they're in prison."

Brian, Julie and Mark Taylor

Vocabulary check

adopt (v) adoption (n) – when a family takes a baby to keep and look after
birth mother / father – the real mother / father of an adopted child
bring up – look after and raise
legal action – using the law to get what you want
give yourself up – take yourself to the police to be arrested
trial – the process where criminals are sent to prison (if they are guilty)
he was sentenced (to) – he was told how long he had to stay in prison
prison – the place where criminals are sent
deception – when you tell a lie or give wrong information

Key task

You have one of three newspaper articles about the same story. The other students have got different newspapers. **Tell your group the name of your newspaper.**

All three newspapers have got some mistakes about the facts in the story. In your group **you must ask questions** to correct all the mistakes. If two of the three newspapers agree on a fact, it is correct. There are 15 mistakes in total. Good luck! Here is a question to start with:

When did Brian and Julie adopt Mark?

Note: YOU CAN'T SHOW YOUR ARTICLE TO THE OTHER STUDENTS!

Discussion

- Do you think that Brian and Julie deserved to go to prison?
- How do you think their son feels towards his birth father, Andrew?
- Do you think Andrew did the right thing? What else could he have done?
- Why didn't Brian and Julie tell Mark about the adoption? Do you think this was a mistake?

In Actual Fact

Text B

☆ THE SAN FRANCISCO DAILY STAR ☆

In 1979 Brian and Julie Taylor from New York adopted a son and called him Mark. Mark's birth mother, Donna McGee, gave up the child on the advice of her father. Unfortunately, Mark's birth father, Andrew Rocco, didn't know she had had a baby. He wasn't married to Donna at the time. Mr Rocco wanted to bring up the baby himself, so he began legal action to get his son back. Brian and Julie already loved Mark and were worried about losing him. So they ran away with their baby to New Mexico. They changed their names to Barry and Karen Fowler. For nearly 20 years they lived in New Mexico, a happy, friendly family with a big secret. Then in 2001, Mark applied to be a police officer and the police discovered that their name was false. Brian decided to give himself up to the police. The trial took almost two years. Brian and Julie were told to pay $100,000 to Mr Rocco, who had spent the money looking for his lost son. Brian Taylor was sentenced to two years in prison for kidnapping and his wife Julie did not go to prison.

After the trial Mark said about Mr and Mrs Taylor, "These are two people I love very much. Now I'm just glad that it's all over."

Brian, Julie and Mark Taylor

Vocabulary check

adopt (v) adoption (n) – when a family takes a baby to keep and look after
birth mother / father – the real mother / father of an adopted child
bring up – look after and raise
legal action – using the law to get what you want
give yourself up – take yourself to the police to be arrested
trial – the process where criminals are sent to prison (if they are guilty)
he was sentenced (to) – he was told how long he had to stay in prison
prison – the place where criminals are sent
kidnap – take a child illegally

Key task

You have one of three newspaper articles about the same story. The other students have got different newspapers. **Tell your group the name of your newspaper.**

All three newspapers have got some mistakes about the facts in the story. In your group **you must ask questions** to correct all the mistakes. If two of the three newspapers agree on a fact, it is correct. There are 15 mistakes in total. Good luck! Here is a question to start with:

When did Brian and Julie adopt Mark?

Note: YOU CAN'T SHOW YOUR ARTICLE TO THE OTHER STUDENTS!

Discussion

- Do you think that Brian and Julie deserved to go to prison?
- How do you think their son feels towards his birth father, Andrew?
- Do you think Andrew did the right thing? What else could he have done?
- Why didn't Brian and Julie tell Mark about the adoption? Do you think this was a mistake?

In Actual Fact

Text C

THE CHICAGO SUN

In 1979 Brian and Julie Taylor from New York adopted a son and called him Mark. Mark's birth mother, Donna McGee, gave up the child on the advice of her doctor. Unfortunately, Mark's birth father, Andrew Rocco, didn't know about the adoption. He wasn't married to Donna at the time. Mr Rocco wanted Donna to bring up the baby, so he began legal action to get his son for Donna. Brian and Julie already loved Mark and were worried about losing him. So they ran away with their baby to New Mexico. They changed their names to Barney and Helen Powers. For over 20 years they lived in New Mexico, a happy, friendly family with a big secret. Then in 2001, Mark was arrested by a police officer and the police discovered that their name was false. Brian decided to give himself up to the police. The trial took almost a year. Brian and Julie were told to pay $100,000 to Mr. Rocco, who had spent the money on legal fees. Brian Taylor was sentenced to 12 years in prison for kidnapping and his wife Julie received six months.

After the trial Mark said about Mr and Mrs Taylor, "These are two people I love very much. Now I'm just glad that it's all over."

Brian, Julie and Mark Taylor

Vocabulary check

adopt (v) adoption (n)	– when a family takes a baby to keep and look after
birth mother / father	– the real mother / father of an adopted child
bring up	– look after and raise
legal action	– using the law to get what you want
give yourself up	– take yourself to the police to be arrested
trial	– the process where criminals are sent to prison (if they are guilty)
legal fees	– the cost of legal action
he was sentenced (to)	– he was told how long he had to stay in prison
prison	– the place where criminals are sent
kidnap	– take a child illegally

Key task

You have one of three newspaper articles about the same story. The other students have got different newspapers. **Tell your group the name of your newspaper.**

All three newspapers have got some mistakes about the facts in the story. In your group **you must ask questions** to correct all the mistakes. If two of the three newspapers agree on a fact, it is correct. There are 15 mistakes in total. Good luck! Here is a question to start with:

When did Brian and Julie adopt Mark?

Note: YOU CAN'T SHOW YOUR ARTICLE TO THE OTHER STUDENTS!

Discussion

- Do you think that Brian and Julie deserved to go to prison?
- How do you think their son feels towards his birth father, Andrew?
- Do you think Andrew did the right thing? What else could he have done?
- Why didn't Brian and Julie tell Mark about the adoption? Do you think this was a mistake?

5 E-mail Madness: Teacher's notes

Topic focus	E-mail and the internet; Computers; Buying and selling
Grammar / Functional focus	Question forms; Asking for information; Making arrangements
Level / Number of students	Intermediate to Upper intermediate / Minimum four students
Time	30–40 minutes (Extension 10 minutes)
Additional skills	Increasing writing speed / writing e-mails

Preparation

Copy worksheets A and B (one per pair), and the extra e-mail sheet including the computer time race (two per pair). Cut up the extra e-mail sheet as indicated.

1 Suggested lead-in

Write the following questions on the board for discussion in pairs (5 mins): *How often do you write e-mails? Who do you usually write them to? Why? Do you often attach things? What? Why do you think e-mails have become more popular than letters?*

2 Introducing the task

Hand out the worksheet, one per pair, giving worksheet A to all the pairs on one side of the classroom and worksheet B to the pairs on the other side.

Note: *The number of A pairs should be equal to the number of B pairs in the classroom, so if necessary, make some groups of three students.*

Students read the instructions. Check that they understand what their e-mail address is (A pairs: nerdmonster21@yahoo.com / B pairs: crazyhorse 707@hotmail.com).

Each pair will be writing exclusively to another pair in the classroom, so decide which pairs will be writing to each other, but don't tell them. (*see picture*)

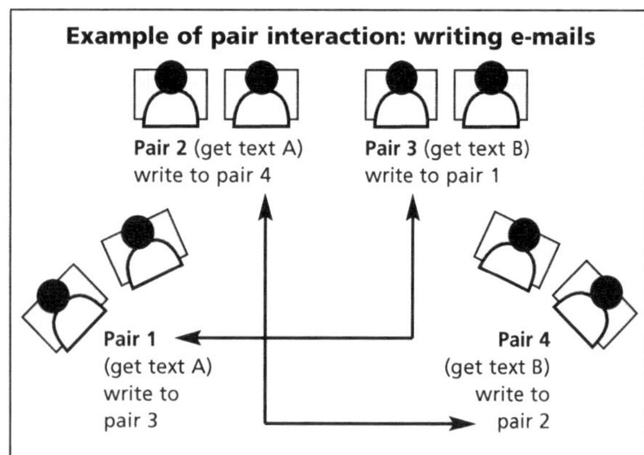

3 Writing the first e-mail

Give them three to four minutes to write their first e-mail. Monitor and keep them working quickly. Collect in the e-mails, remembering whose is whose.

4 Continuing the correspondence

Now tell the students a new e-mail has just arrived in their inbox and give the e-mails out, *taking care to give the right e-mails to each pair*, so that each A pair swaps e-mails with a B pair. Students read the e-mails they have just received. Hand out another blank e-mail to each pair and give them three minutes to write their response. Collect in and redistribute the messages to the same pairs. Continue handing out, collecting in and redistributing e-mails until they have brought the correspondence to an appropriate conclusion.

Note: *Some teams will finish more quickly than others, realising that they need to meet up to complete the transaction. Get these teams to role play the meeting in groups of four. Put the following stages on the board as a guideline for the role play:*

- *Introduce yourselves.*
- *Inspect the computers, check for any problems.*
- *Discuss the prices, try to agree.*
- *Conclude the conversation and say goodbye.*

5 Round up

Put the pairs together for a quick chat, discussing the following questions: *Was it easy to understand the e-mails? Were you confused about anything? Was there anything you found difficult to say in English?*
Find out which pairs got the computer they wanted.

6 Extension: Computer Time Race

Hand out the quiz to groups of three to four students. Give them only five minutes to answer all the questions. Check the answers at the end.

Answers

1 Possible answers: mouse, monitor (screen, display, VDU), keyboard, printer, scanner, webcam, joystick, modem, hard disk drive, CD ROM, CD rewriter (CD burner) floppy disk drive, processor or CPU, etc.
2 a) print a document b) re-boot the computer c) scan for a virus d) click on an icon e) paste an image
3 a) T b) F (documents are stored on the hard disk drive or C drive) c) T d) F (floppy disks hold up to 1.5Mb uncompressed) e) F (at the time of writing) unless you download something or click on an .exe file.
4 H – Dell S – Microsoft S – Norton H – HP (Hewlett Packard) S – Adobe
5 1 – open your internet browser; 2 – log onto hotmail; 3 – write an e-mail; 4 – attach a photo; 5 – send the e-mail.

E-mail Madness

Your e-mail address is: nerdmonster21@yahoo.com

You have seen the following advert on a website for second-hand computers.

For sale:
Nearly new desktop PC – Dell 3400
Complete with flat screen monitor, keyboard and mouse. 30 GB hard drive, Pentium 4, Windows XP, lots of games for free!
Price: £750 o.n.o.
Email: crazyhorse707@hotmail.com

You are interested in buying this desktop computer. Write an e-mail to the address shown, asking any questions you need to ask before you buy the computer. When you get the reply, you will need to meet up to collect and pay for the computer.

By the way, you are also selling this laptop computer. Somebody might contact you regarding it. You need to sell your current computer to get the money to buy the new one. Make sure you get enough money to buy the one you want.

For sale:
Laptop Computer – Sony A 101
Really nice silver laptop. Only one year old.
With CD Rewriter and printer.
Processor – 256Mhz. Price: £780 o.n.o.
Email: nerdmonster21@yahoo.com

Write your e-mail message below. Make sure you write your return address. Then tear off the e-mail and 'send' it by handing it to your teacher.

tear here

File Edit View Format Tools Message Help

To:

From:

Subject:

E-mail Madness

Your e-mail address is: crazyhorse707@hotmail.com

You have seen the following advert on a website for second-hand computers.

For sale:
Laptop Computer – Sony A 101
Really nice silver laptop. Only one year old.
With CD Rewriter and printer.
Processor – 256Mhz. Price: £780 o.n.o.

Email: nerdmonster21@yahoo.com

You are interested in buying this laptop computer. Write an e-mail to the address shown, asking any questions you need to ask before you buy the computer. When you get the reply, you will need to meet up to collect and pay for the computer.

By the way, you are also selling this desktop computer. Somebody might contact you regarding it. You need to sell your current computer to get the money to buy the new one. Make sure you get enough money to buy the one you want.

For sale:
Nearly new desktop PC – Dell 3400
Complete with flat screen monitor, keyboard and mouse. 30 GB hard drive, Pentium 4, Windows XP, lots of games for free!
Price: £750 o.n.o.

Email: crazyhorse707@hotmail.com

**Write your e-mail message below. Make sure you write your return address.
Then tear off the e-mail and 'send' it by handing it to your teacher.**

tear here

File Edit View Format Tools Message Help

To:

From:

Subject:

File Edit View Format Tools Message Help

To:

From:

Subject:

File Edit View Format Tools Message Help

To:

From:

Subject:

E-mail Madness: Computer Time Race

You have five minutes to complete the following tasks. Good luck!

1 Name five parts of a computer:

a) *mouse* b) ____________

c) ____________ d) ____________

e) ____________

2 Match the verbs with the nouns:

a) print	an icon
b) re-boot	a document
c) scan for	an image
d) click on	the computer
e) paste	a virus

3 Write T for true and F for false:

a) A modem is used for connecting your computer to the internet.

b) A processor is the place where you save documents or files on your computer.

c) All notebooks have LCD monitors.

d) You can get over 20 megabytes onto a floppy disk.

e) You can get viruses from browsing the internet.

4 Which of the following companies mainly make software (write S), and which mainly make hardware (write H)?

___ Dell ___ Microsoft ___ Norton

___ HP (Hewlett Packard) ___ Adobe

5 Put these stages in the correct order:

___ write an e-mail

___ attach a photo

___ open your internet browser

___ log on to Hotmail

___ send the e-mail

6 We're in Business! : Teacher's notes

Topic focus	Business; Work; Restaurants; The Internet; Animals
Grammar / Functional focus	Future tenses; *going to* and *will*; 1st Conditional structures
Level / Number of students	Upper intermediate to Advanced / Minimum six students
Time	45–60 minutes (Extension 30 minutes)

Preparation

Copy the three texts in equal numbers, so that each student gets a copy of either A, B or C.

1 Suggested lead-in

Write the following questions on the board for discussion in pairs (5 mins): *Would you like to start your own business? What would you do? How would you start it going?* Get some feedback.

2 First reading in original groups

Divide the class into three groups of equal numbers. Give out a different text to each group. Students read the text (5–7 mins.). Optional global reading task: *Do you think the idea will be a success?*

3 Vocabulary check

Ask the students to match the words and definitions. Each group can check their answers together.

Answers
Text A 1e 2f 3b 4a 5g 6d 7h 8c
Text B 1c 2e 3f 4b 5g 6a 7h 8d
Text C 1d 2h 3c 4g 5b 6a 7f 8e 9j 10i

4 Jigsaw exchange stage

Re-organise the groups so that each new group includes at least one student who has read each of the three texts. Students ask and answer the key questions in their new groups, explaining vocabulary if necessary. Monitor. As the groups finish, move them on to the discussion questions.

Answers
Text A 1 A karaoke restaurant where diners vote for the best singers to get a free meal. **2** Sing For Your Supper! **3** Voting and a free meal are original, but karaoke restaurants are now quite common. **4** Refurbish the premises, get a loan, hire a compere. **5** Experience in the music industry – no problem finding a good compere. **6** Worried about karaoke going out of fashion, but confident that the restaurant can be changed if necessary.
Text B 1 A travel company organising animal encounters (swim with dolphins, etc.) **2** Close Encounters. **3** Some companies offer these experiences locally, but this company brings them to UK customers. **4** He/She has to travel to locations, negotiate aspects of holidays and must also decide if clients are going to enjoy holidays or not. **5** Experience as a vet helps her choose holidays, and also ensure that the animals don't suffer from too many tourists. **6** He/She is worried about price (keeping costs down for young customers), and animal welfare (see 5).
Text C 1 A website where English students can meet friends. **2** e-friend.com **3** Several such sites are around now, but a few years ago it was original. **4** He has to think up quizzes / exercises for the site, and get more money from investors. **5** As a teacher of English, he can write online quizzes and activities. His friend has computer skills. **6** He's worried about service – will it be free? This depends on revenue from advertising, which depends on the number of hits.

5 Class feedback

Once all the groups have completed the key questions and the discussion stage, bring the class together, checking difficult / interesting answers. They will probably want to know which of the ideas was successful. Tell them that the businesses were all started in 2001. One of them went bankrupt in the first six months (e-friend). One of them is still surviving, but has changed (Sing For Your Supper. It's now a jazz bar!) One of them is now very successful, has made millions and is still expanding (Close Encounters). Get them to guess which is which!

Extension: We're in Business! Group Project

Preparation

Copy the task sheet (one per group of three to five students) and the Bank Manager role play sheet (one per group).

Method

Divide the students into groups (three to five), and hand out the task sheet. Read through it with them and let them begin. Tell them all to work in the same currency (dollars or pounds). Keep to the time limits.

Tip: Tell them to draw on their individual areas of experience and expertise, to inspire good ideas.

Five minutes before the role play, take one student from each group to play the bank manager for another group. Put all the bank managers together and give them the bank manager role play sheet. They should work together to write more questions. After five minutes, start the role plays. At the end get the bank managers to tell the whole class how it went, how much money they wanted, and whether they got it or not.

We're in Business!

Text A

Lee, 32, Record Producer

"We're planning to open a new restaurant here in London with a karaoke theme. We're going to build the stage right in the middle, with all the tables around it. On each table there will be a special voting button and the diners will be able to vote for the singers that they really like. At the end of each evening, the singer with the most votes will get their meal for free. If someone is really successful we'll invite them back again! We're going to call the restaurant "Sing For Your Supper!"

We've just found the right premises, and the builders are starting next week. It should take about three-four weeks to get the basics done – plumbing, electrics and so on. Then the decorators will move in. We've got enough money for all that, although I expect we'll need another loan to tide us over until the business starts making a profit. Having worked in the music industry, I know a lot of great singers who are interested in the job of compere. We're going to start the auditions next week, which should be fun!

To be honest, my biggest worry is with the karaoke theme. If it stays popular for the next five or seven years, we'll make a lot of money. If it doesn't, we might be in trouble. Fortunately, we've got a good business plan and if the karaoke thing doesn't work out, it'll be easy to convert it into a cabaret type restaurant."

Vocabulary check

1 *stage (n)*	**a)** people who paint walls or put up wallpaper, etc.
2 *premises*	**b)** water systems, including toilets, sinks, etc.
3 *plumbing*	**c)** change the form or function of something
4 *decorators*	**d)** the host of a cabaret, TV show or theatre performance
5 *tide over (v)*	**e)** the raised platform in a theatre or concert hall where the performers stand
6 *compere (n)*	**f)** the accommodation for a business
7 *auditions*	**g)** lend someone money for a short period of time
8 *convert (v)*	**h)** job interviews in the entertainment business (for actors or singers)

Key questions

1 What is the idea?

2 What is the business going to be called?

3 Is the idea original? Why?

4 What does he / she have to do before the business can start operating?

5 What experience does he / she have? How will that help him / her?

6 What things is he / she worried about? How will he / she deal with these problems?

Discussion

- What do you think of the three ideas?
- Do you think they will all be successful?
- Would you change any of them in any way? How? Why?
- Which of the ideas might go out of fashion?
- Which of the ideas is the most original? Why?
- Which would you invest in? Why?

We're in Business!

Text B

Carol, 34, Vet

Close Encounters

"The company's going to be called 'Close Encounters'. It will be like a travel company, but with a difference: we're going to be the first UK company to specialise in holidays for people to spend time with wild animals. For example, they can go to Florida and spend a week diving with wild dolphins, or they can go to Uganda and spend a week with mountain gorillas. They'll also be able to take part in research projects in the Amazon and the Indonesian rainforests, helping on the reserves.

We're going to work from home, so we don't need an office yet. The most important thing to organise is the holidays themselves and the next three months will involve a lot of travelling. Next week I'm going to Brazil to look at the research projects there and to find out what holidaymakers can do and whether they will enjoy it or not. Then I'm flying to Florida to look at the hotels and to try diving with the dolphins. It sounds like a lot of fun, but it also involves a lot of paperwork, negotiation and so on.

My two main worries are the prices and animal welfare. Holidays that include animal experiences are always going to be expensive, but if the prices are too high, we won't be able to attract the young clients that the holidays are designed for. So I've set maximum prices for each holiday, and if the cost goes over that, I won't offer it in the brochure. As for animal welfare, we're a bit concerned about disturbing the animals, some of which are protected. Fortunately, my experience as a vet will help me to make the right decisions. I love animals, and if they start suffering from the tourists, I'll just reduce the numbers on each trip."

Vocabulary check

1 *specialise*	a) interrupt someone / thing (often by making a noise or getting in their way)
2 *reserves (n)*	b) discussion and agreement on prices or conditions in a business deal
3 *paperwork*	c) concentrate on only one area or topic
4 *negotiation*	d) feel pain or discomfort
5 *animal welfare*	e) areas of land where the animals and trees are protected
6 *disturb*	f) documents and letters that have to be written
7 *protected (adj)*	g) animal safety and animal rights
8 *suffer*	h) kept safe (often by law)

Key questions

1 What is the idea?

2 What is the business going to be called?

3 Is the idea original? Why?

4 What does he / she have to do before the business can start operating?

5 What experience does he / she have? How will that help him / her?

6 What things is he / she worried about? How will he / she deal with these problems?

Discussion

- What do you think of the three ideas?
- Do you think they will all be successful?
- Would you change any of them in any way? How? Why?
- Which of the ideas might go out of fashion?
- Which of the ideas is the most original? Why?
- Which would you invest in? Why?

We're in Business!

Text C

Paresh, 27, Teacher of English

"We've got a great idea, and it won't cost us too much either. We're going to set up a website that offers students of English the chance to meet other students and make friends with them. There will be a chat room and a notice board, but most importantly, students will be able to open up special e-mail boxes, where they can write e-mails and send photos to each other. We've already got the domain name: 'e-friend.com'.

I'm setting it up with my friend, Nick, who is a web designer and deals with all the computer stuff. Barring any technical hitches, it's going to take him about two more months to complete the website. Meanwhile, I'm going to be thinking up lots of interactive English language quizzes and exercises. I'll also be dealing with the investors. We probably need about $7,000 to get it up and running. I'm meeting one investor tomorrow, actually.

The main concern we have at this stage is whether we can offer the service to students for free. This will only be possible if we get enough advertising on the site. And that depends on the number of hits we're getting. Advertisers will only pay for space on a frequently visited website, and it'll be a while before we get enough hits to attract advertisers. If we can't get the advertising, we'll just have to charge students $5.00 to join, at least to begin with."

Vocabulary check

1	*set up (v)*	a)	you can take part, not just watch
2	*chat room*	b)	small, temporary problems
3	*domain name*	c)	the name for a website that is also its address (*they start with: www.*)
4	*barring*	d)	start / organise
5	*hitches (n)*	e)	something you worry about
6	*interactive*	f)	people who give money to businesses, and then take part of the profits
7	*investors*	g)	excluding / without
8	*concern (n)*	h)	a place where internet users can 'talk' by writing to each other in real time
9	*hits (n)*	i)	very often
10	*frequently*	j)	visits (to a website)

Key questions

1 What is the idea?

2 What is the business going to be called?

3 Is the idea original? Why?

4 What does he / she have to do before the business can start operating?

5 What experience does he / she have? How will that help him / her?

6 What things is he / she worried about? How will he / she deal with these problems?

Discussion

- What do you think of the three ideas?
- Do you think they will all be successful?
- Would you change any of them in any way? How? Why?
- Which of the ideas might go out of fashion?
- Which of the ideas is the most original? Why?
- Which would you invest in? Why?

We're in Business! Group Project

The Task

In groups of three to five, think up an original idea for a new business. It could be similar to the ideas you read about (e.g. internet web site, new travel idea, restaurant), or it could be a completely different idea.

Stage 1 *10 minutes*

You should think of:

- an original idea to attract the customers
- a good name for your business
- what jobs each of you will do in the company
- a possible location (if necessary)
- what services you are going to offer
- how you will beat the competition

Stage 2 *10 minutes*

Then decide:

- how much money you will need to borrow from the bank
- what you will spend the money on
- how you are going to advertise your product

To make your business plan clear, you could create a flow chart on a piece of paper showing the development of your business over the first year.

Later in the lesson, you will have to 'pitch' your idea to the bank manager. S/he will only give you the loan if s/he is convinced that this is a good idea.

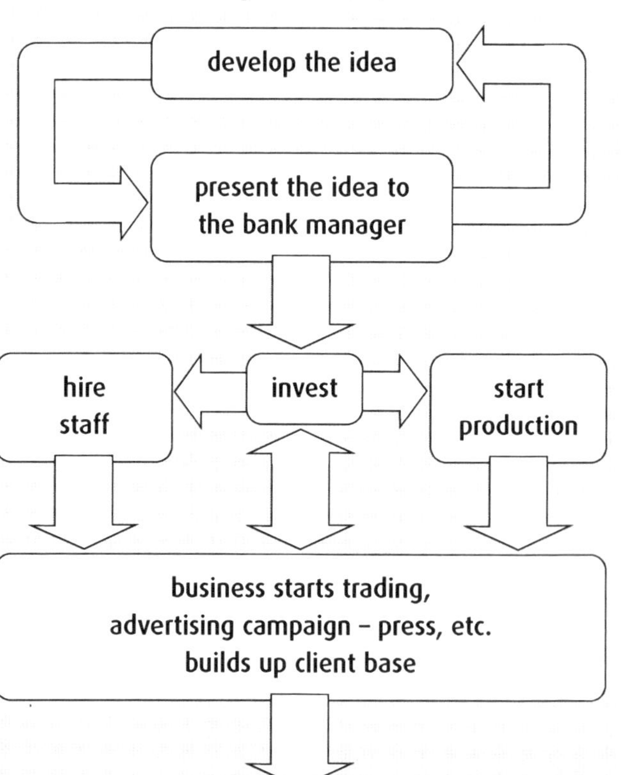

Stage 3 *10 minutes*

Interview with the Bank Manager

Present your idea to the bank manager. Try to be professional, using your flow chart and explaining it carefully and clearly. Make sure you cover all the points you discussed in stages 1 and 2.

Your aim is to get the necessary money for the business.

Remember: the bank manager will want to see a profit from the company as soon as possible, so you must make it clear how much money you expect to make and when you expect to start making a profit.

We're in Business!

Bank Manager Role Play

You must play the role of the bank manager. You will have ten minutes to interview one of the groups of students. Your aim is to decide if you are prepared to lend them the money for their business or not!

- First, find out exactly how much money they want.
- Then ask them to explain their business idea.
- Listen carefully to their idea and ask lots of questions.

Here are some suggestions. Add some more:

Interview questions

Why do you think you will succeed?
What exactly do you need the money for?
How are you going to advertise?
What will you do if you don't reach your first-year goals?
How soon will we see a profit?
Have you done any market research?
What problems are you prepared for?
If all goes well, how do you plan to expand?

____________________?
____________________?
____________________?
____________________?

- When they have finished, tell them if you will lend them the money or not. You may choose to lend them less than they ask for, or you may request that they change one or two points in their idea.
- After the interview has finished, tell the rest of the class about the business idea, and tell them if they got the money or not.

We're in Business!

Bank Manager Role Play

You must play the role of the bank manager. You will have ten minutes to interview one of the groups of students. Your aim is to decide if you are prepared to lend them the money for their business or not!

- First, find out exactly how much money they want.
- Then ask them to explain their business idea.
- Listen carefully to their idea and ask lots of questions.

Here are some suggestions. Add some more:

Interview questions

Why do you think you will succeed?
What exactly do you need the money for?
How are you going to advertise?
What will you do if you don't reach your first-year goals?
How soon will we see a profit?
Have you done any market research?
What problems are you prepared for?
If all goes well, how do you plan to expand?

____________________?
____________________?
____________________?
____________________?

- When they have finished, tell them if you will lend them the money or not. You may choose to lend them less than they ask for, or you may request that they change one or two points in their idea.
- After the interview has finished, tell the rest of the class about the business idea, and tell them if they got the money or not.

7 Mystery Movie Star: Teacher's notes

Topic focus	Films; Celebrities and celebrity gossip
Grammar / Functional focus	Modal verbs of deduction (*might, could, can't* etc.); Direct and reported speech; Past simple passive
Level / Number of students	Upper intermediate to Advanced / Minimum six students
Time	30–50 mins, depending on number of teams (Extension 20–25 mins.)

Preparation

Copy the Movie Star fact sheets (one per team of two to three students) and Movie Pitch – The Project (*below:* one per team). If you can get hold of any celebrity magazines, such as 'Hello' or 'OK', take them in to the lesson.

1 Suggested lead-in

Elicit the names of ten international movie stars. Write them on the board, along with the following questions for pair discussion (5 mins): *How many of the movie stars are Hollywood stars? Why do you think Hollywood dominates the film industry? Why do you think film star gossip sells so many magazines and newspapers?* Get feedback and continue the discussion by looking at celebrity magazines if you have taken some into the class.

2 Preparation for the task

Put the students into teams of two to three (at least three teams). If you have over 18 students, make two groups. Tell them that each team is going to receive some interesting facts about a famous movie star but that **they must keep the identity of the star secret**. Hand out the Movie Star fact sheets. Read through the instructions with them. Give them two to three minutes to decide on the best order to read out their facts. While they're working, put team names and points columns on the board for scoring.

Note: *If the students have recently studied modal verbs of probability / deduction, encourage them to use these verbs during the activity (It might / must / can't be Brad Pitt... etc.)*

Tip: *Use background music and space the teams out so that they can't hear each other's conversations.*

3 The task

Arrange the seating so that all the teams can see and hear each other. Taking it in turns, the teams should read out one fact about their movie star. The other teams should make notes. At the end of the first round (i.e. when all the teams have read out one fact), ask them if they would like to guess the identity of anybody else's star (a wrong guess loses them 20 points). Encourage them to say why they think it is this star. If no one guesses correctly, give all the teams ten points. Then move on to the next round. The longer they stay in, the more points they accumulate. When a team guesses another team's movie star, they get 30 bonus points. Any team that has been knocked out can still listen and try to guess the other movie stars. The rounds continue until all the movie stars have been guessed. At the end, if any stars are left unguessed, the other teams can all have a free guess. The team with the most points wins.

Tip: *Encourage the students to listen to each other carefully and to ask questions or re-phrase if necessary. Do not echo what they say yourself. This will discourage them from listening to each other.*

At the end, if there's time, get each team to summarise two or three of the most interesting facts about their movie star to the class.

Extension: Movie Pitch

Ask them: *If you were a movie screenplay writer, which of the film stars would you most like to write a film for?* Put them into groups of three to four so that they are all writing for a film star they like. Hand out the Movie Pitch Project Sheet (*below*), one copy per group and read through it. If students would prefer, they could write for a different star as long as they know plenty about him / her. Each group should have the fact sheet for their star, and a secretary to make notes. Monitor, offering ideas if needed. After 10–15 minutes get each team to present their idea to the class.

Movie Pitch – The Project

In teams of three to four you have ten minutes to think up an idea for a film for a famous movie star. To ensure that the movie star and the producers are interested, follow these guidelines:

- use some ideas from the movie star's life
- make sure that there are at least two other big stars in the film
- make sure that there is a 'happy ending' for your chosen movie star

Prepare to present your idea to the rest of the class. You may want to draw a few quick pictures for your presentation. Try to make your presentation brief but memorable. (Imagine you are 'pitching' the idea to your chosen star!)

Mystery Movie Star

Here are ten facts about a famous film star. KEEP THE FILM STAR SECRET! You will read them out to other students, and they will try to guess who the film star is. *You can choose which one to read out first, second, etc.* You should try to stop them from guessing the film star for as long as possible, so leave the easy facts until the end. Explain any difficult vocabulary if necessary. *Do not read out the information in brackets.*

Tom Cruise

- His second wife was a famous movie star who often acted alongside him. (Nicole Kidman)
- He was ranked third in *Empire* magazine's list of the top 100 movie stars of all time.
- His attitude to filmmaking changed after he worked with Paul Newman, and he began to make anti-war films, instead of action movies.
- At 14 he was studying to become a priest.
- Both of his two children are adopted.
- For one film and its sequel, he made a record $145 million. (*Mission Impossible 1 & 2*)
- He left his second wife for a woman with a similar surname to his. (Penelope Cruz)
- In 2002 he went home after opening the Oscar Award Ceremony to watch the rest of it on TV with his kids.
- The film that brought him overnight fame was about the pilot of a fighter plane. (*Top Gun*)
- He was born on 3rd July, 1962.

Key vocabulary

alongside – next to, with
ranked – in a position, in an order
adopted – children raised as your own
sequel – a second or third film in a series
overnight fame – instant fame

Points scoring

+10 points for each round if nobody guesses your star.
+30 points extra if you guess someone else's movie star.
-20 points if you guess wrongly!

Don't forget to keep a record of your points total!

Mystery Movie Star

Here are ten facts about a famous film star. KEEP THE FILM STAR SECRET! You will read them out to other students, and they will try to guess who the film star is. *You can choose which one to read out first, second, etc.* You should try to stop them from guessing the film star for as long as possible, so leave the easy facts until the end. Explain any difficult vocabulary if necessary. *Do not read out the information in brackets.*

Bruce Lee

- His real name was Lee Jun Fan.
- He died at the age of 32.
- He spoke four languages. (Cantonese, Mandarin, English and Japanese)
- He once said, "Simplicity is the last step of art."
- He gave dancing lessons to pay for the ship that took him to the USA.
- He used to charge $275 per hour for private lessons. (in Kung Fu)
- He was a quarter German and three-quarters Chinese.
- His last film was called *Game of Death*.
- His voice is only heard in his last film, because all his previous films were dubbed.
- Despite numerous fights throughout his life, he only lost one – when he was 13!

Key vocabulary

charge (v) – ask for or get money for services or products
dubbed (dub) – with a different voice added on later, often in another language
numerous – many

Points scoring

+10 points for each round if nobody guesses your star.
+30 points extra if you guess someone else's movie star.
-20 points if you guess wrongly!

Don't forget to keep a record of your points total!

Mystery Movie Star

Here are ten facts about a famous film star. KEEP THE FILM STAR SECRET! You will read them out to other students, and they will try to guess who the film star is. *You can choose which one to read out first, second, etc.* You should try to stop them from guessing the film star for as long as possible, so leave the easy facts until the end. Explain any difficult vocabulary if necessary. *Do not read out the information in brackets.*

Marilyn Monroe

- Her real name was Norma Jean Mortensen.
- She was abandoned by her mother who went mad.
- She first married at 16.
- Officially, she died of a drug overdose.
- Her natural hair colour was brown.
- She posed naked for *Playboy* magazine.
- She was a direct descendant of a US President. (James Monroe)
- She received less than $1000 each for over half her films.
- She once said, "Dogs never bite me. Just humans."
- Her last film was written by her husband.

Key vocabulary

abandoned – left for ever
drug overdose – too many drugs
naked – without clothes
descendant – children, grandchildren, etc

Points scoring

+10 points for each round if nobody guesses your star.
+30 points extra if you guess someone else's movie star.
-20 points if you guess wrongly!

Don't forget to keep a record of your points total!

Mystery Movie Star

Here are ten facts about a famous film star. KEEP THE FILM STAR SECRET! You will read them out to other students, and they will try to guess who the film star is. *You can choose which one to read out first, second, etc.* You should try to stop them from guessing the film star for as long as possible, so leave the easy facts until the end. Explain any difficult vocabulary if necessary. *Do not read out the information in brackets.*

Charlie Chaplin

- He was born in England.
- He was very famous for his moustache.
- In his first year of filmmaking he made 35 films.
- He had eleven children by four wives.
- He was 36 years older than his last wife.
- He once entered a look-alike contest, dressed as himself, and finished third!
- He very rarely spoke in his films.
- He had deep blue eyes but few of his fans knew this.
- One of his biggest fans was a famous political dictator. (Adolf Hitler. He copied Chaplin's moustache.)
- He was the only person to have written, directed, produced and starred in his own film.

Key vocabulary

moustache – hair between the nose and the mouth
look-alike contest – a competition where the aim is to look like somebody well-known or famous
rarely – not very often
star in – be one of the leading actors in (a film)

Points scoring

+10 points for each round if nobody guesses your star.
+30 points extra if you guess someone else's movie star.
-20 points if you guess wrongly!

Don't forget to keep a record of your points total!

Mystery Movie Star

Here are ten facts about a famous film star. KEEP THE FILM STAR SECRET! You will read them out to other students, and they will try to guess who the film star is. *You can choose which one to read out first, second, etc.* You should try to stop them from guessing the film star for as long as possible, so leave the easy facts until the end. Explain any difficult vocabulary if necessary. *Do not read out the information in brackets.*

Julia Roberts

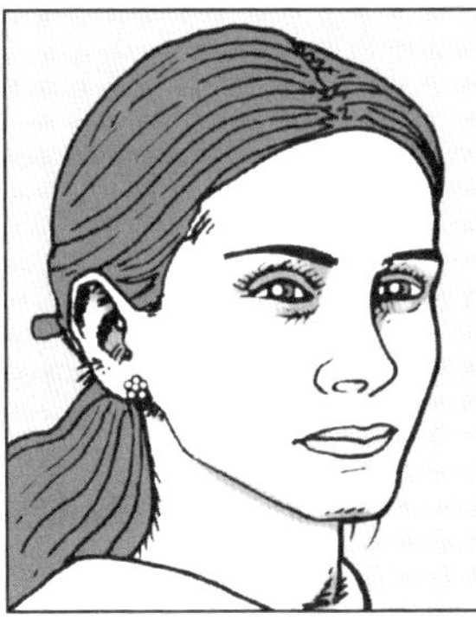

- She was born in Smyrna, Georgia in 1967.
- She is a qualified vet.
- She played the role of a prostitute in her first big film. (*Pretty Woman*)
- She does a lot of work for the charity UNICEF.
- Her first husband was a country music singer. (Lyle Lovett)
- In 2002, she was the highest paid actress in movie history.
- She lies on her back to have her make-up applied before going onto a film set – she insists it gives her a relaxed look.
- She has dated over ten famous actors and broken off two engagements.
- She has never acted in a sequel.
- In her acceptance speech for the Oscar she won, she forgot to thank the person the film was named after! (*Erin Brockovich*)

Key vocabulary

charity – an organisation created to help people or animals
applied – (here) put on make-up
insists (insist) – demand something forcefully
sequel – a second or third film in a series
acceptance speech – speech you give after winning a prize

Points scoring

+10 points for each round if nobody guesses your star.
+30 points extra if you guess someone else's movie star.
-20 points if you guess wrongly!

Don't forget to keep a record of your points total!

Mystery Movie Star

Here are ten facts about a famous film star. KEEP THE FILM STAR SECRET! You will read them out to other students, and they will try to guess who the film star is. *You can choose which one to read out first, second, etc.* You should try to stop them from guessing the film star for as long as possible, so leave the easy facts until the end. Explain any difficult vocabulary if necessary. *Do not read out the information in brackets.*

Sharon Stone

- She has an IQ of 154 and is a member of Mensa.
- She was a model before she became an actress.
- She is famous for clothes that she didn't wear for one scene. (during *Basic Instinct*)
- She posed naked for *Playboy* magazine.
- Her first big break was in a science fiction film with Arnold Schwarzenegger. (*Total Recall*)
- Her adopted son is called Roan.
- Her most famous role was as a bisexual psycho called Catherine Tramell. (in *Basic Instinct*)
- She is allergic to caffeine.
- She once said she would be the next Marilyn Monroe.
- She once said you shouldn't have a relationship with anybody who has more problems than you do.

Key vocabulary

Mensa – an organisation for very clever people
naked – without any clothes
big break – first chance to succeed
adopted (adopt) – child raised as your own
psycho – (psychopath) someone who is violent and mad
allergic – when the body reacts badly to something

Points scoring

+10 points for each round if nobody guesses your star.
+30 points extra if you guess someone else's movie star.
-20 points if you guess wrongly!

Don't forget to keep a record of your points total!

8 Chicken Tonight! : Teacher's notes

Topic focus	Food; Cooking; Recipes
Grammar / Functional focus	Imperatives for giving instructions; Countable and uncountable nouns
Level / Number of students	Intermediate to Upper intermediate / Minimum four students
Time	20–30 minutes (Extension 15 minutes)

Preparation

Copy the worksheet (one per group of two to three students) and the extension activity below (one per group).

1 Suggested lead-in

Write the following questions on the board for students to discuss in small groups (5 mins): *How good are you at cooking?* (beginner – advanced) *What are your favourite recipes?* Pre-teach (lower levels): *(chicken) breast; sakè (Japanese rice wine); leeks; parsley; breadcrumbs; flour; gherkins; mixture.*

2 Starting the task

Tell the students that they are going to receive the recipes for two chicken dishes mixed up, and that the first team to sort out the recipes correctly will be the winners. Hand out the worksheets and read through the instructions with them. Make sure they understand how to number the stages (T1, T2, T3, etc. for Teriyaki; K1, K2, K3, etc. for Kiev). Monitor carefully to check they are doing it correctly. It usually takes eight to twelve minutes.

3 As the teams finish

As the teams finish, check their worksheet. If they have made any mistakes let them know how many, but don't tell them where. Accept the first correct worksheet and give the other groups three more minutes to finish. Check the answers.

Answers
Reading down the worksheet, the stages should read: K1, T3, K3, T5, K7, T1, K2, T2, K6, T4, T6, K4, T7, K5

4 Discussion

Tell the students to discuss the five questions on the worksheet (5 mins). Get some feedback at the end, finding out what dishes they described and why they like them.

Suggestion: *Some of the students (or you) could prepare the dishes to taste in a future lesson. Alternatively, the students could all bring in a favourite dish from their country.*

Extension: Chicken Piri-Piri

Tell the students that you are going to give them the list of ingredients for another famous chicken dish, but this time they have to decide on the recipe themselves. Hand out the ingredients list (*below*). Give them five to ten minutes. At the end ask each group to read out their stages, then tell them who was closest and hand out the original recipe (*below*).

Note: *If several or all of your students are Portuguese, you could do this with another dish. Just give the students the list of ingredients!*

Have a look at the recipe below. It is for a Portuguese dish. Read the ingredient list carefully and discuss how you think it is prepared. Write the stages down on a piece of paper. There are seven stages in total.

Chicken Piri-Piri

Some Portuguese would say that this is their national dish. It is quite easy to prepare and very tasty! Piri-Piri are small red peppers. They are very hot!

Serves four
Preparation time: 40 minutes

Ingredients:
4 chicken breasts
50g garlic
2 red chilli peppers (Piri-Piri)
2 red peppers
15ml olive oil
200ml dry white wine
100g black olives
To serve: parsley, fresh white bread and dry white wine

Chicken Piri-Piri – Correct Recipe

1. Cut the chicken breasts into thin pieces. Chop the garlic and the peppers. Don't forget to take the seeds out of the chilli peppers. **2.** Heat the olive oil in a frying pan. Add the chicken pieces and fry over a high heat for 2 minutes. Take the chicken out of the pan.
3. In the same pan, fry the garlic and peppers until soft. Add the wine and bring to the boil. **4.** Now return the chicken to the pan, add the olives and some salt and pepper. **5.** Over a low heat, fry the mixture for about 15 minutes. **6.** Chop the parsley carefully and sprinkle on the dish just before you serve it. **7.** Serve the dish with fresh white bread, parsley and dry white wine.

Chicken Tonight!

Below are the ingredients and the stages of the recipes for two different chicken dishes, one from Japan and one from Ukraine.

- First read the ingredients lists carefully
- Then decide which recipe each stage belongs to (write ***T*** for Teriyaki, ***K*** for Kiev)
- Number the stages in the correct order (the first have been done – ***T1***, ***K1***)
- The first team to finish are the winners! Good luck!

Ingredients – Chicken Teriyaki

chicken
rice
leeks
sakè
sugar
soy sauce
cucumber
spring onion

Ingredients – Chicken Kiev

chicken
garlic
lemon skin
mixed herbs
butter
salt & pepper
flour
eggs
breadcrumbs
oil

Discussion Questions

1. Have you ever tried either of the dishes?
2. Which do you think is healthier? Why?
3. Which is easier to prepare? Why?
4. Which do you think you would prefer? Why?
5. Think of a chicken dish that you like. Describe it, including the ingredients and the stages in the recipe.

K	1	Chop the garlic and mix with the lemon skin in a bowl. Chop the herbs and add to the bowl.
		Fry the chicken breasts on each side for three minutes over a high heat. Take the chicken out of the pan.
		Freeze the garlic butter for 30 minutes. Meanwhile cut a small pocket into each chicken breast. Don't cut through the pieces.
		Put the fried chicken back in the pan with the sauce and cook for two more minutes. Meanwhile, in another pan, fry the chopped leeks for about four minutes until soft.
		Serve the chicken with the new potatoes, sliced lemon and pickled gherkins.
T	1	Wash the rice and put it in a pan to boil for 20 minutes. Wash and slice the leeks.
		Add the butter to the bowl and a little salt and pepper to make garlic butter. Mix well.
		Don't remove the skin from the chicken, just cut each breast three or four times so that it will fry quickly.
		Heat plenty of oil in a frying pan, add the chicken breasts and fry over a medium heat for eight to ten minutes on each side.
		In the same pan, mix the sake and sugar over a low heat and bring to the boil. Add the soy sauce and cook over a high heat for six minutes, until the sauce is ready.
		Cut the cooked chicken and put it onto a plate. Serve with the leeks and the rice.
		Remove the garlic butter from the freezer and put about 40g of it into each piece of chicken. Put the breasts in the fridge and leave them there for $1\frac{1}{2}$ hours.
		Chop the cucumber and spring onion and arrange around the chicken. Serve with Japanese beer or sakè.
		Later, put the flour, the eggs and the breadcrumbs into three separate dishes. Dip each piece of chicken first in the flour, then in the egg, then in the breadcrumbs.

9 The Natural Solution: Teacher's notes

Topic focus The environment; Farming / Agriculture; Culture and history

Grammar / Functional focus The passive voice; Mixed tenses, Contrasting past and present

Level / Number of students Upper intermediate to Advanced / Minimum three students

Time 40–50 minutes (Extension 25 minutes / Crossword 7 minutes)

Preparation

Copy the three texts (one text per student). Check that there is a map of the world in the class before the lesson.

1 Suggested lead-in

Pre-teach: *plantation, erosion, soil, deforestation, harvest, pesticides, ecosystem, intensive / organic farming.* Using the map, ask the students to find: the Philippines, El Salvador, Burkina Faso. Ask them: *What do you think these three countries are like? Think about: climate / plants and animals / people / agriculture.*

2 First reading in original groups

Divide the class into three groups of equal numbers. Give out text A to the students in group 1, text B to group 2 and text C to group 3. Students read the text (5–7 mins). They can also do the vocabulary check in pairs / threes. Monitor carefully.

Answers
Text A 1c 2d 3h 4e 5i 6b 7a 8f 9g **Text B** 1d 2g 3a 4b 5h 6i 7e 8c 9f **Text C** 1c 2e 3g 4a 5b 6i 7f 8j 9d 10h

3 Jigsaw exchange stage

Re-organise the groups so that each new group includes at least one student who has read each of the three texts. Students ask and answer the key questions, explaining vocabulary if necessary. Monitor. As the groups finish, move them onto the discussion questions.

4 Class feedback

Having completed the key questions and the discussion stage, check difficult / interesting answers as a class.

Answers – Key questions
Text A 1 Loss of soil fertility, caused by rain erosion. **2** Oxfam suggested building long stone lines (3,000-year-old method). **3** Lines help rain to soak into land, reducing erosion. Requires stones (found locally). **4** Crops, trees, etc. have started to grow again. People are able to live off the land. **5** Yes. To thousands of other farmers. **6** Birds, animals and insects have returned, and the desert is being pushed back. **7** (suggested answer) Look into your history to solve current problems.
Text B 1 Deforestation for intensively-farmed coffee plantations set up by huge multinationals. **2** To use shade coffee plantations – a traditional solution supported by the Rainforest Alliance. **3** Trees above the coffee support a variety of other animals and plants / diversity of plant types reduces erosion and improves water quality. The scheme requires support from coffee companies. **4** It has allowed small-scale local farmers to improve wages and living conditions. **5** Yes, to over 1,000 other families. **6** 188 bird species, 31 mammals, 26 reptiles and 326 tree / bush species recorded on farms. **7** (suggested answer) What's good for the plants and animals is also good for the people.
Text C 1 Coral reefs have died off due to dynamite fishing, over-fishing and cyanide poisoning. **2** To set aside a sanctuary on the reef and return to traditional fishing practices, suggested by Silliman University scientists. **3** Fish are able to thrive in the sanctuary, repopulating surrounding reefs. The sanctuary requires careful management and protection from locals. **4** Fishing catches have doubled. Benefits from tourism are also noticeable. **5** Yes. Neighbouring islands have also adopted similar projects. **6** Reefs become protected as sanctuaries, as do animals that live on the reef. **7** (suggested answer) Protect the environment and it will protect you.

Answers – Discussion
Similarities include: Influence of western technology / intensive farming as source of problem; Population growth as another factor; Use of traditional ideas to solve problems; Support of science and organisations from developed countries to solve problems; Local people taking initiative and responsibility for their own environment; Local people realising that protecting the environment also protects their livelihood.

Extension – Project Ichar

Preparation

Copy and cut up the project sheets and the information cards (one set per group of three to four students).

Method

Divide the class into groups of three to four students and give them the Project Ichar sheet. Students read the sheet. Then hand out the possible solutions: one or two to each student. Tell the students to summarise the solutions to their group, discuss the options and decide what should be done, both immediately and over the next three to five years (10–15 mins). Get feedback at the end and compare the different solutions and their relative merits.

Revision Crossword

Use the crossword in a subsequent lesson for revision of vocabulary. Hand out the crossword (one per group of three). Check the answers after five minutes.

Answers
Across: 2 sediment **3** rocks **4** sanctuary **6** biodiversity **8** rob **9** coral reef **Down: 1** erosion **2** sustainable **5** nutrients **6** bush **7** species

The Natural Solution

Text A

In Burkina Faso, on the southern edge of the Sahara Desert, the local people are using a traditional method to make the deserts green with crops and trees again.

The Problem

After many years of population increase earlier this century, the people watched the once-fertile land turn into desert. Too many trees were cut down for firewood and unnatural western crops, which robbed the soil of its nutrients, were being used. When the rain came, it was so heavy that it ran off the land quickly, taking the topsoil and leaving hard-packed salt and sand. Gradually the harvest began to fail, the people left, the animals, birds and insects disappeared and the Sahara Desert moved in. "We thought we had lost our village and our home. We were preparing to move south to the city," explained Ninda, a local farmer.

The Solution

With the help of Oxfam*, the local villagers were encouraged to look into their history for help. A three-thousand-year-old method was recovered that was beautiful in its simplicity. "We tried building long stone lines using local rocks. Some people thought it was crazy, but we tried it anyway," recalls Ninda. The stone lines stop the rain from running off the soil, even where the land seems flat. Over the years the lines get blocked up naturally with sediment and become more effective. In addition they reduce wind erosion and are natural places to plant trees, which also combat erosion.

The Result

Within just a few years, areas with stone lines were coming back to life. The trees started to grow again and the crops produced a good harvest. Birds, animals and insects gradually returned and the environment was restored. Neighbouring villages saw the results and also started to build stone lines. Now thousands of farmers are using the technique and the desert is gradually being pushed back. "For the first time in ten years, I saw parrots in the trees last year," Ninda smiled. "It's like the good old days again."

**Oxfam is a large international charity supporting the development of third world countries*

Vocabulary check

1 *fertile*	**a)** fight with
2 *nutrients*	**b)** when soil is removed by wind or rainwater
3 *topsoil*	**c)** able to make plants grow
4 *harvest (n)*	**d)** 'vitamins' in the soil
5 *sediment*	**e)** when the crops are gathered
6 *erosion*	**f)** put back
7 *combat (v)*	**g)** a type of tropical bird (*see picture*)
8 *restored*	**h)** the top layer of earth where plants grow
9 *parrots*	**i)** soil or mud left behind by water

Key questions

1. What was the problem? What was it caused by?
2. What solution was suggested? Who by? Where did it come from?
3. How does it work? What does it require?
4. What effect has it had? How have people benefited?
5. Has it spread?
6. How has the ecosystem benefited?
7. Is there a moral to the story?

Discussion

What similarities can you find in the three accounts? Think about...

- the cause of the problem
- the role of traditional methods in the solution
- the role of scientific research in the solution
- the moral to the story

Have you ever heard of any similar environmental problems, in your country for example? What happened?

The Natural Solution

Text B

In El Salvador, the return to traditional coffee farming techniques is benefiting both small, local farms and the environment.

The Problem

Over the last 50 years over 70% of Central American rainforest has been cleared, much of it for intensively-farmed coffee plantations. This is a tragedy in an area with some of the richest ecological biodiversity in the world. These intensive plantations are the creation of huge multinational coffee companies. They involve the removal of all other plant species except for coffee and are farmed using chemical pesticides and fertilisers. They become biological deserts, supporting less than 5% of the animals, birds and plants that lived here before. What's more, local farmers are forced to work on these large farms for less than a dollar a day, losing their livelihood and their independence.

The Solution

As early as 1930, it was noted that traditional shade coffee plantations (plantations which allow other species of tree to grow with the coffee, providing the shade that natural coffee requires) support almost as many species of birds and mammals as rainforests do. With support from organisations such as the Rainforest Alliance and several coffee companies, local farmers were encouraged to return to shade coffee as a greener alternative.

The local farmers are paid good prices for their coffee in return for growing the coffee according to the guidelines set out by the Rainforest Alliance.

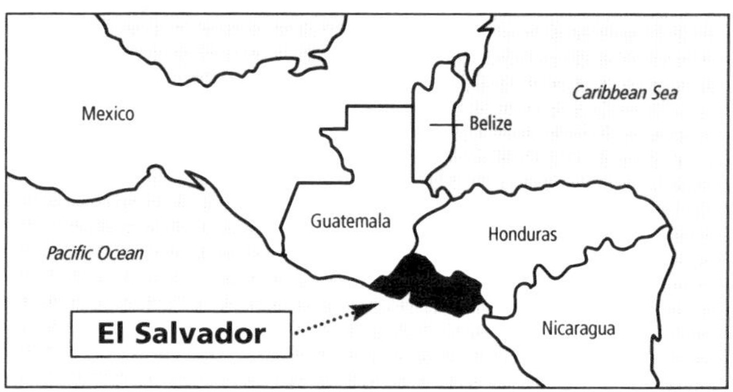

Shade plantations have the added advantage of being sustainable (the soil quality remains high and rich in nutrients), thus reducing erosion and improving water quality.

The Result

Over 1000 farm families have now benefited from the scheme and are improving wages and living conditions. Incredibly, 188 species of birds, 31 species of mammals, 26 species of reptiles and 326 tree and bush species have been recorded on the shade coffee farms involved in the scheme. They are providing a vital biological corridor between the two most important national parks in El Salvador.

The coffee is now being sold in the USA and Europe as shade plantation certified, ensuring that over 100 million American and 200 million European coffee drinkers can now contribute directly to the health of the rainforest environment in Central America.

Vocabulary check

1 *biodiversity*	a) chemicals to make the plants grow faster
2 *pesticides*	b) source of income / work
3 *fertilizers*	c) when soil is removed by wind or rainwater
4 *livelihood*	d) the variety of wild animals and plants
5 *shade*	e) 'vitamins' in the soil
6 *guidelines*	f) one type of animal
7 *nutrients*	g) chemicals that kill insects, etc.
8 *erosion*	h) not in direct sunlight
9 *species*	i) advice or rules to follow

Key questions

1 What was the problem? What was it caused by?

2 What solution was suggested? Who by? Where did it come from?

3 How does it work? What does it require?

4 What effect has it had? How have people benefited?

5 Has it spread?

6 How has the ecosystem benefited?

7 Is there a moral to the story?

Discussion

What similarities can you find in the three accounts? Think about...

- the cause of the problem
- the role of traditional methods in the solution
- the role of scientific research in the solution
- the moral to the story

Have you ever heard of any similar environmental problems, in your country for example? What happened?

The Natural Solution

Text C

In the Philippines, Apo Island is providing a model for sustainable fishing in harmony with the environment.

The Problem

The Philippines is home to almost 10% of the world's coral reefs. Sadly, over the last 40 years, a large increase in population has caused fishermen to abandon traditional fishing techniques. The use of dynamite to blast fish out of the water, and cyanide to poison and capture fish for aquariums, has led to the death of many of the coral reefs. Attempts to create marine sanctuaries by governmental organisations were unsuccessful, because the fishermen, who still needed to feed their families, ignored the sanctuaries.

The Solution

In 1985 scientists from Silliman University managed to get the agreement of the 500 local residents of Apo Island to create a marine sanctuary on the island's reefs. It was agreed that if, after two years, the sanctuary was not benefiting the community, it would be removed. The locals were sceptical, but took the initiative in deciding where the sanctuary borders would be and how the sanctuary would be managed and protected. They also agreed that only traditional spear fishing methods could be used in the area around the sanctuary.

The Result

After two years fishing catches had doubled in the waters around the sanctuary. Not surprisingly, all the residents of Apo Island had become strong supporters of the scheme. They guarded their area carefully and stopped any illegal fishing by neighbouring fishermen. What's more, the reefs became so beautiful that the island started to benefit from tourism. Two resorts with dive shops were built, providing further employment and other technological benefits. Of course, neighbouring islands quickly adopted similar Coastal Resource Management Projects (CRMPs) and set up similar community-based sanctuaries.

"The community still faces some issues that need to be resolved," observes Mercy Teves, a local government worker. "But," Rupert Sievert says, "Apo Island can show the benefits, to both the natural ecosystems and the community that depends on them, of consistent and sustained protection."

Vocabulary check

1 *sustainable*	a) catch
2 *coral reef*	b) a place where the animals and plants are protected
3 *abandon (v)*	c) able to continue or keep going
4 *capture (v)*	d) protect something by keeping watch over it
5 *sanctuary*	e) a tropical underwater habitat
6 *sceptical*	f) lead the decision-making
7 *take the initiative*	g) (*here*) stop using
8 *spear (n)*	h) (*here*) begin to use
9 *guard (v)*	i) unwilling to believe an idea or opinion
10 *adopt*	j) a type of weapon (*see picture*)

Key questions

1. What was the problem? What was it caused by?
2. What solution was suggested? Who by? Where did it come from?
3. How does it work? What does it require?
4. What effect has it had? How have people benefited?
5. Has it spread?
6. How has the ecosystem benefited?
7. Is there a moral to the story?

Discussion

What similarities can you find in the three accounts? Think about...

- the cause of the problem
- the role of traditional methods in the solution
- the role of scientific research in the solution
- the moral to the story

Have you ever heard of any similar environmental problems, in your country for example? What happened?

The Natural Solution

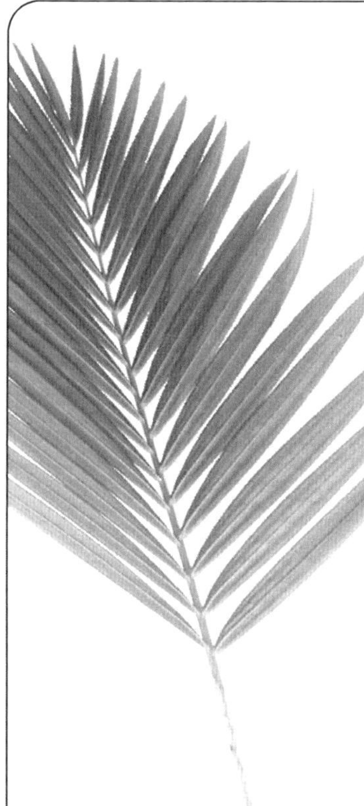

Project Ichar

You work for an international agricultural aid organisation, Agriworld.

You have been called to the mountain village of Ichar in Northern India, where the locals are facing serious problems. Most of these problems are due to the overuse of non-traditional farming techniques including intensive rice cultivation (30% of land use) and tea plantations (40% of land use).

The problems are:

- poor soil quality – traditional crops have difficulty growing
- soil erosion – caused by rainfall on deforested hillsides
- illness among the people of the village – caused by chemical pesticides and fertilisers getting into the drinking water
- loss of local wildlife – frogs, lizards, birds and fish have declined since pesticides became common
- increase in pesticide-resistant insects – reducing crop harvests

You will each receive one of several *possible* solutions to the problems. Summarise the solution to the group and discuss the advantages of each. Try to agree on what must be done immediately, and make notes on a basic three to five year plan for the village.

The Natural Solution

Project Ichar

You work for an international agricultural aid organisation, Agriworld.

You have been called to the mountain village of Ichar in Northern India, where the locals are facing serious problems. Most of these problems are due to the overuse of non-traditional farming techniques including intensive rice cultivation (30% of land use) and tea plantations (40% of land use).

The problems are:

- poor soil quality – traditional crops have difficulty growing
- soil erosion – caused by rainfall on deforested hillsides
- illness among the people of the village – caused by chemical pesticides and fertilisers getting into the drinking water
- loss of local wildlife – frogs, lizards, birds and fish have declined since pesticides became common
- increase in pesticide-resistant insects – reducing crop harvests

You will each receive one of several *possible* solutions to the problems. Summarise the solution to the group and discuss the advantages of each. Try to agree on what must be done immediately, and make notes on a basic three to five year plan for the village.

The Natural Solution – Project Ichar: Information cards

1 Re-forestation using a fast-growing imported species of tree

This tree is useful for stopping erosion. It is cheap and fast-growing, but is not natural to the area and it can kill off natural species. This would be a good short-term solution.

4 Frog breeding programme to increase the natural defence against insect crop damage

Frogs are one of the most important natural predators of crop-damaging insects, and this programme would be set up in the village, with the frogs being gradually released back into the fields. A cheap solution, although the frogs may be poisoned by the pesticides in the soil.

2 Re-forestation using mixed natural forest

This is a slow process. The seeds have to be grown in the village. Once they are planted, the trees need to be protected from sheep and goats. Expensive, but a good long-term solution.

5 Building mud walls to reduce erosion

This is a slow, expensive process. Wood is needed (from trees), and all the materials have to be carried up the hills. Once in place, the walls are effective, but can break in heavy rain.

3 Changing back to traditional crops in mixed fields

The traditional method of agriculture, using grains, vegetables and fruits which can be eaten directly by the villagers. The mixed fields mean that the soil quality slowly increases. The problem is that the villagers cannot get very good prices for these crops at the local markets, unlike tea or rice.

6 Banning of all pesticides and fertilisers

This is dangerous, as there are not enough natural predators of the insects (e.g. frogs, birds and lizards) and crops might fail. In a neighbouring village, crops started to grow well only after three years of organic farming.

The Natural Solution – Vocabulary Revision Crossword

How many of the words can you remember? They all appeared in one of the three texts.

Clues Across →

2 soil or mud left behind by water (8)
3 another word for (large) stones (5)
4 a place where the animals and plants are protected (9)
6 the variety of wild animals and plants (12)
8 steal (3)
9 a tropical underwater habitat (5,4)

Clues Down ↓

1 when soil is removed by wind or rainwater (7)
2 able to continue or keep going (11)
5 'vitamins' in the soil (9)
6 a small tree (4)
7 one type of animal (7)

10 Room 101: Teacher's notes

Topic focus Likes and dislikes; Society and culture

Grammar / Functional focus Expressing strong emotion, especially dislikes; Conditionals, especially 2nd conditional

Level / Number of students Intermediate to Advanced / Minimum four students

Time 15–20 minutes (Extension 20–30 minutes)

Preparation

Copy the Room 101 worksheet (one per student). The extension activity can be cut off if you would like to do it in a separate lesson.

1 Suggested lead-in

Write the 2nd conditional question from the worksheet on the board: *If you could send the things you really, really hate to a room where they would disappear forever, what things would you choose?* Briefly explain the concept of Room 101. (It comes from George Orwell's novel *1984* and is a place where all the things we hate are kept.) Tell them one or two things you would send to Room 101. Use abstract ideas as well as objects to demonstrate what can be sent (eg rudeness; alarm clocks) and get a couple of suggestions from them. Save the main discussion for later in the lesson.

2 Reading

Ask the students to read about the three choices made by Kevin Wilson. Tell them to try to guess what the three things are, and to write a suggested title for each paragraph in the space provided. Get feedback after five minutes, eliciting different suggestions.

Original Answers
1 Mobile phone ring tones **2** Computers that don't work **3** Foreign tourists on the Tube

3 Vocabulary check

Ask the students to match the underlined words in their text to the definitions beneath the text.

Answers 1c 2i 3a 4h 5g 6e 7b 8d 9f

4 Discussion

Tell the students to answer the questions as a speaking exercise in pairs or threes.

5 Class feedback

Check the answers. Draw the students' attention to the variety of language used by Kevin to express his feelings. If necessary, write one or two of the expressions on the board and provide more examples as to how they could be used. Have a quick vote on which of Kevin's ideas should go into Room 101.

Extension: What would you send to Room 101?

Now is the time when the students can come up with their own nominations for Room 101. If you used the Suggested lead-in, the students may already have some ideas. Put them into groups of three to four and tell them they are now going to think up their own suggestions for Room 101. Read through the instructions with them and start them off. Monitor. Before you start the presentations, tell each group to decide who will present which idea. The students should come out to the front of the class for the presentations to ensure that everyone can see and hear them. After each group has finished get the whole class to vote on each one by a show of hands. A majority vote sends the choice to Room 101!

Suggestion: *This Room 101 idea can be an enjoyable, cathartic tool for use in class, allowing students to let off steam whenever they need to. You could create a Room 101 suggestions list where students can write up nominations. Do the presentations and voting every few weeks.*

Room 101

If you could send the things you really, really hate to a room where they would disappear forever, what things would you choose?

Kevin Wilson, comedian and writer, makes his choices...

As you read, write a title for each paragraph in the space:

1 ______________________________

"What's wrong with the good, old fashioned 'ring, ring'? Why is it necessary for phones to play the tune to La Bamba or Mozart's Horn Concerto? If I wanted to listen to music, I would buy a CD player! And I really hate it when someone plays you their latest ring tone and expects you to be impressed by it. There should be a law against people using stupid ring tones in public!"

2 ______________________________

"It's not so much the things themselves, it's when they crash! You get this feeling of complete helplessness. You try Control, Alt, Delete a few times and it doesn't work, and then you just wait and pray. Then, if the computer doesn't work, you have to call for help, and the call usually costs about £1 per minute. That's when I get really irritated, because they always take so long to explain things. Once I had to take my computer to be repaired, and after two weeks they told me: "We can't do anything! I hope you've backed up your files on CD." I hadn't!"

3 ______________________________

"It's one of the few things that annoys me almost every day here in London. As far as I'm concerned, tourists should be banned from using the Tube in the rush-hour! They walk so slowly, in big groups, and always stop and wait in the really busy places, like at the top of escalators! And when they get to the ticket gates, they always take about five minutes to find their tickets, and when they do find them, they put them in the wrong side and complain when the gate doesn't open. It gets me really angry! I have probably missed about 30 trains because of tourists."

Vocabulary check

1 *tune*
2 *be impressed by*
3 *crash*
4 *helplessness*
5 *irritated*
6 *back up (v)*
7 *banned*
8 *the Tube*
9 *ticket gates*

a) break down / stop working
b) made illegal
c) melody
d) underground railway (British English)
e) save a second copy
f) machine that checks your ticket
g) annoyed, angry
h) a feeling that no one can help
i) really like someone or something they've got

Discussion

1. Why does Kevin hate these three things?
2. What examples does he give for each choice?
3. Do you agree with all his choices? Why? / Why not?
4. If you agree, can you think of any more examples from your own life?
5. If you disagree, what would you say to keep the choice out of Room 101?
6. Which of the choices does he seem most angry about?
7. What expressions does he use to show his anger?
8. Do you think he's joking about any? How do you know?

Room 101

What would you send to Room 101?!?

Work in groups.

Preparation

First spend about ten minutes thinking of suggestions for Room 101. Note down your ideas.

Then choose two or three ideas and prepare to tell the rest of the class about them.
Make sure you...

- say why it should go to Room 101
- give examples or tell a quick story to show what you mean
- can convince the other students that it is a good suggestion
- decide who is going to present the suggestions

Presentations

Now present your ideas to the class. All the students should listen carefully to the suggestions. At the end, you will vote for the best three ideas. Only these three will go to Room 101.

Useful language

I can't stand...	It really annoys / irritates me when...
It gets me really angry...	I get so wound up when...
I am amazed at...	As far as I'm concerned...
You get this feeling of...	What I really hate is...
Why do we bother (doing)... ?	What's the point in (doing)... ?

11 Raining Cats and Dogs: Teacher's notes

Topic focus	Idioms and proverbs; History; Traditions
Grammar / Functional focus	Past simple; Expressing habitual past actions (*They would..., People used to...*)
Level / Number of students	Upper intermediate to Advanced / Minimum six students
Time	30–45 minutes (Revision Extension 10 minutes)

Preparation

Copy the worksheet opposite (1 per student), and the idiom origin cards (1 set per class). Cut up both sheets as indicated.

1 Suggested lead-in

Write the following sentence on the board and the questions below for discussion in pairs (5 mins): *Rock music isn't my cup of tea; I prefer jazz or classical. 1) What is the idiom in this sentence? 2) What do you think it means? 3) What do you think is the origin of this idiom? 4) Do you have a similar idiom in your language?* Tell the students that they are going to learn about some idioms with far more puzzling or surprising origins.

2 Matching exercise (A)

Hand out the worksheet (make sure you've cut off the bottom section) and tell them to match up the sentences, working in pairs. Monitor (6–8 mins.) and then check the answers.

Answers 1c 2i 3a 4e 5j 6b 7h 8g 9d 10f

3 Deducing the meaning (B)

In pairs the students try to guess from the context what the underlined idioms mean. Do the first one with them. Check the answers after five to seven minutes. See the idioms origins sheets for brief answers.

4 Teacher example (C)

Tell the students that you are going to tell them three possible explanations of the origin of the idiom 'raining cats and dogs' (*see opposite*). They should listen and then decide which they think is the correct one. Tell the stories naturally.

Answer
Although all three explanations have been put forward, the second (surprisingly) is closest to the truth. The earliest written reference in the 17th century was to it raining 'dogs and polecats' after a particularly serious bout of the plague.

5 Preparation stage (D)

Put the students into groups of 2 to 4 (minimum 3 groups). Read through D on the worksheet with them, asking each group to choose one of the idioms. Give them the idiom origin card for that idiom. Two different groups cannot choose the same idiom. Tell them that this is the true explanation of the origin of the idiom, and give them ten minutes to think up two more false origins. Tell them that later they will have to present their three explanations to the other students, who will try to guess which one is true. Monitor carefully, providing suggestions and vocabulary.

Tip: The three explanations should sound similar when presented, using the same level of English and register. Encourage them to rewrite the true story in their own words to make it sound more like the two false ones (e.g. include one or two errors or simpler expressions.)

6 Call my bluff (E)

The groups take it in turn to come to the front of the class and present their three versions. Suggest that a different student reads each version. The other groups have 30 seconds to decide which is true. Score 1 point to each team that guesses correctly and 3 points to the 'home' team if none of them guess correctly.

Tip: During the presentations, make sure that they are all listening carefully. Insist that they all put their pens down, stop any whispering and bring them as close together as possible.

7 Round up

Find out which idioms have equivalents in the students' first language(s). If they're interested, they could also read about the remaining idioms.

Revision extension

Best done in a subsequent lesson. Make sure they can't see the original idioms. Students do A in pairs (4 mins.). Check the answers. Allow six minutes for B. Get feedback, eliciting different opinions.

Answers
A 1 *to* Greece **2** *another* feather **3** *under* the weather **4** *on* the grapevine **5** Touch wood **6** worth *his* salt **7** raining cats and dogs **8** out *of* the bag **9** straight *from* the horse's mouth **10** *on her* sleeve.
B 5 and 8 are inappropriately used.

Raining Cats and Dogs

A Match sentences 1 to 10 with the sentence from the box that follows most naturally.

1 I think we're going to have to call off the picnic.

2 If Andy told you, don't believe it.

3 If Nigel told you, it must be true.

4 I hear you've been chosen to run the new advertising campaign.

5 Susan isn't coming in to work today.

6 Since the operation, my knee has felt much stronger.

7 Joe's an outstanding golf player.

8 I was a bit reluctant to spend so much on a laptop computer.

9 Don't tell Nicola about Gavin's surprise party.

10 She's just like her sister when it comes to relationships.

a) He gets it straight from the horse's mouth.

b) Touch wood.

c) It's raining cats and dogs outside.

d) She's bound to let the cat out of the bag.

e) That's another feather in your cap.

f) She wears her heart on her sleeve.

g) But it really turned out to be worth its salt.

h) I'm quite good, but I couldn't hold a candle to him.

i) He picks things up on the grapevine.

j) She's feeling a bit under the weather.

B Working in pairs, try to guess the meaning of the underlined idioms and expressions.

C Some idioms in English seem very strange! This is because they have very unusual or very old origins. Your teacher will read out three different explanations of where the expression 'raining cats and dogs' came from. Try to decide which is the true explanation.

D Now, in teams, choose one of the other idioms that you have just learnt. Your teacher will give you a text explaining the true origin of the idiom. Read it and then invent two more (false) explanations of where the idiom came from. Later in the lesson you will read out your explanations to the other students in your class and they will try to guess which is the true one. Your aim is to make them believe one of the *false* explanations.

E Take it in turns to present the different versions of the origin of your idiom to the other students. If another team guesses which is the correct one, they win one point. If none of the teams guess correctly, your team wins three points!

Raining Cats and Dogs – The three explanations

1 *Hundreds of years ago English people used to have thatched roofs on their houses. (A thatched roof is made from thick layers of dried grass.) During the winter, the roof was the warmest place in the house. The pets of the house knew this, and they would often climb onto the roof and under the thatch to keep warm. Unfortunately for the animals, when it rained heavily the thatch would get wet and very slippery and the animals would often fall. So we started to use the expression to refer to times when the rain was particularly heavy.*

2 *During the 16th and 17th centuries in London, especially at times when there was an outbreak of the plague, many animals died from the disease. Heavy rains would often make the situation worse. At such times, dogs, cats and other animals, which weren't taken away like human victims, would litter the streets, and if the rain was strong enough, they would be carried along in the drains, even falling into rivers, giving the impression that they had fallen with the rain.*

3 *Raining cats and dogs comes from a rare French word,* catadoupe, *meaning waterfall, which was often used, both in France and later in England by French landowners to refer to heavy rainfall. The English farmers who worked on the land did not, of course, speak French, but they learnt the expression, gradually changing it to 'cat a dog' and then 'cats and dogs'.*

"on the grapevine"

meaning

A way of getting information through gossip or rumours.

origin

In the 1850s in the USA, just after the telegraph had been invented, hundreds of miles of telegraph lines were being built every day. In 1859, a man called Colonel Bee tried to save time by using trees to carry the lines, instead of wooden poles. The trees continued growing and the wires stretched and broke, hanging down to the ground like grapevines. During the American Civil War Colonel Bee's telegraph became a joke, and they used the expression to refer to inaccurate messages or misinformation.

"touch wood" or "knock on wood"

meaning

With luck. We use the expression when we want or need good luck.

origin

This expression, which started as "knock on wood" and then developed to "touch wood", dates back hundreds of years to medieval times, when people believed that evil spirits lived in trees. These spirits, people believed, enjoyed ruining our day, so whenever people talked about what they hoped or wanted in the future they would knock on the nearest tree, or other wooden object, so that the evil spirits inside couldn't hear what they were saying and bring bad luck.

"a/the feather in your cap"

meaning

An achievement or success, often one that wins you favour with someone important.

origin

In North America, when a native American Indian fought well in battle, acting bravely or killing an enemy, they received an eagle's feather to add to their <u>headdress</u>. The feathers were like medals for the Indians, and the more feathers they had in their headdress the more status they had within their tribe.

"can't hold a candle to (someone)"

meaning

To be much worse at doing something than someone else.

origin

Before electric lights, if someone needed to do something important in the dark, such as a doctor performing an operation, or a musician playing a difficult piece of music, they needed a helper to hold a candle to provide light while they worked. Holding the candle is, of course, an easier job. Even so, the person who held the candle still needed to understand a little about what the doctor needed to see, and therefore the job was often done by an apprentice. To say that one man cannot hold a candle to another is like saying that he is not even good enough to be his apprentice.

"worth its salt"

meaning

To be very useful, worth paying for, or a useful person / employee

origin

During the time of the Romans, salt was extremely useful, both for preserving meat and to make food taste better. But it was also very rare. Many Roman soldiers received some salt as part of their pay (the word 'salary' comes from the Latin 'salarium', meaning 'of salt') and it is probably among the Romans that the expression was first used. When the Romans said that a soldier was worth his salt, they meant that he was worth his salary, i.e. a useful soldier.

"to let the cat out of the bag"

meaning

To tell a secret to the wrong person.

origin

During medieval times, baby pigs (piglets) were usually sold tied up in bags. This was a way of keeping the animals calm and stopping them from escaping. If you opened the bag, the piglet would often jump out and run away. Some dishonest traders would catch cats, put them in the bag and sell them as piglets. Thus, letting the cat out of the bag means revealing a secret to the wrong person.

"under the weather"

meaning

Ill or sick, usually temporarily.

origin

The phrase comes from the time when sea travel was more common than today. At sea, when there is a storm, the waves get bigger and the passengers often feel sea sick. During a long storm, it was the custom to explain that somebody was absent from dinner or another social occasion because they were 'under the weather', meaning sick.

"wearing your heart on your sleeve"

meaning

To show all your emotions and feelings.

origin

The expression dates back to one of William Shakespeare's plays, *Othello*, in which one of the characters says: "I will wear my heart upon my sleeve". The character was using the expression to mean that he would pretend to be open about his emotions, telling *Othello* everything he felt in order to deceive and eventually destroy him. Although this usage is slightly different from the modern one, the expression developed and became more general in meaning over time.

"straight from the horse's mouth"

meaning

A way of getting information directly from the source – often important, private information.

origin

In the past, people who sold horses (called *traders*) would often pretend that a horse was much younger, stronger and healthier than it really was, yet the best way to find out about these things is to look inside the horse's mouth. Its teeth will tell you its age and general health. If its lips are cut or damaged, they can tell you if it is an aggressive horse that has been kept on a tight *rein*. Only if you could persuade a trader to let you see inside the mouth would you know the true health of the horse.

rein – the strap a rider puts in a horse's mouth and behind the neck to control it

Raining Cats and Dogs

Raining Cats and Dogs

Revision Activity

A) Each of the following idioms has a small mistake (e.g. wrong word, word missing, etc.). Find them and correct them!

1. If you're looking for a nice, quiet beach holiday, Spain can't hold a candle for Greece.
2. If I succeed with this business deal, it will be the other feather in my cap and could lead to promotion.
3. I remember Craig very well. He was always feeling below the weather with colds or the flu.
4. I heard the grapevine that you're getting engaged. Congratulations.
5. I can't believe it. The flight has been delayed by two hours! Touch the wood.
6. When we took him on, he didn't have very much experience, but he turned out to be worth some salt.
7. That umbrella isn't going to help you today. It's raining with cats and dogs outside.
8. This weekend I'm going to let the cat out the bag and buy a new car.
9. You can believe Julie. She works as the mayor's secretary and gets it straight out of the horse's mouth.
10. Don't worry if she starts crying. She always wears her heart in a sleeve.

B) Look again at the above sentences. two of the idioms have been used in the wrong context. Which two? Why are they wrong?

12 Stabbed in the Back: Teacher's notes

Topic focus	Crime (murder); Courts and trials; Love and affairs
Grammar / Functional focus	Past simple and Past continuous tenses; Question forms; Various functions: Expressing emotion, Agreeing and disagreeing
Level / Number of students	Upper intermediate to Advanced / Minimum seven students
Time	60–90 minutes (2 lessons possible); (Extension 30 minutes)

Preparation

Copy the synopsis sheet (1 per 2 students) and the role play cards (1 of each per group of 7–16 students). Cut up as indicated. Take sticky tape, pieces of paper (1 per student, for name badges) and a knife (murder weapon) to class. In a previous lesson, you could teach related vocabulary: *defendant, prosecuting counsel, jury, stand trial, plead,* etc. and tell them how (jury) trials work in the UK. If possible, use a classroom with moveable furniture, and plan in advance how you can best rearrange the room to simulate a courtroom.

***Note:** This activity is better suited to some cultures than others. If you are unsure about using it, discuss it with students first, or watch a TV drama or film extract based on a trial that would lead in to the activity. If you are unsure about how trials work in the UK, you could adapt the activity to use the system of the USA or the students' country.*

1 Organising the students and allocating roles

Decide before the lesson who is going to play each role in the drama. (If you are going to split the activity up over two lessons, make sure that the main characters will be present for both lessons.) Seven main roles should be played by students: 1) Mrs Wilson, the defendant; 2) Mr Carmichael, primary witness; 3) prosecuting counsel; 4) defending counsel; 5) Dr Simms, pathologist; 6) Mrs Patel, neighbour; 7) Mr Hislop, Mrs Wilson's lover. Additional roles include: two more counsels (thus making two lawyers on each side), judge (played by a student or the teacher) and optional jury (3–12 students). The optimum number of students is from 7 to 13. If you have over 13, make two smaller groups. Allocate the key roles to outgoing students who would make good actors, and choose fluent, analytical students for the lawyers (they do the most talking).

2 Preparation for the trial

Hand out the task sheet and give them all six to eight minutes to read it. Check any difficult vocabulary. Tell the students which roles they will be playing and hand out the role cards. Make name badges for the important roles and stick them on with sticky tape. Group the students to prepare for the trial. Group 1: Defending counsel, Mrs Wilson, Mrs Patel and Mr Hislop. Group 2: Prosecuting counsel, Mr Carmichael, Dr Simms. Tell them to work together to prepare for the trial. The role cards for the two counsels indicate clearly what they should do during this preparation time. Allocate 20–30 minutes for preparation. If there are students playing other, neutral roles (e.g. judge and jury), get them to reorganise the room. Then they can discuss the questions on the Jury role card.

3 Organising the trial

The Judge role card has a suggested order for events in the trial. It is the judge's job to ensure that this order is followed and to decide on time periods for each stage of the trial. Allocate from 30 minutes (approx. 2–3 mins. per stage) to 45 minutes (3–4 mins. per stage) for the whole trial.

4 The trial

This can take place in the same or a subsequent lesson. Make sure that the room is organised appropriately. The more props, the better! Make sure that the counsels know how to object and the judge knows how to sustain or overrule objections; this can make the trial really fun! The judge should begin by calling for order in court, and then follow the stages on her / his role card. If you are not playing the judge, take the role of a court clerk and 'assist' the judge in case s/he forgets to do anything important! Students usually get into their roles very well, and the only things to watch are the time allocations.

5 Rounding up the trial

At the end, the judge / jury should give their verdicts and pass sentence. If the judge / jury are unsure about the guilty / not guilty verdict, let them see the definitions of Murder and Manslaughter from the Counsel for the defence / prosecution role cards. Lead a chat for a few minutes about how it went, what the key stages in the trial were, and what was most challenging linguistically.

***Extra Idea:** If you have a video camera available, and the students don't mind, why not video the whole trial? They will really enjoy watching their performances.*

Extension: Trial report

This can be done for homework (individual reports), or in class (groups of 2–3 students). Tell the students to imagine that they were newspaper journalists at the trial and that, having been there, they must write an article, reporting the trial for their newspaper (150–250 words), trying to make it both interesting and dramatic. Make sure they give their articles a headline.

Stabbed in the Back

On the 24th of November last year, Mrs Wilson stabbed her husband with a knife, killing him. But was it a mistake, or murder?

Mr and Mrs Wilson had been married for three years. The marriage was not a happy one. Mrs Wilson had had several affairs, often receiving lovers at their family home. Mr Wilson had, at least twice, beaten his wife severely. On one of these occasions she went to hospital and the police were involved. No charges were pressed. Approximately three months before the stabbing, Mrs Wilson began seeing her latest lover, Mr Hislop. The relationship was probably kept a secret from Mr Wilson until the 24th of November.

On the 24th of November, Mr Wilson returned home from work on his lunch break with his colleague, Mr Carmichael. While Mr Carmichael waited outside, Mr Wilson entered the house, and found Mrs Wilson and Mr Hislop in bed together. A fight immediately followed in the bedroom between Mr Hislop and Mr Wilson. Mr Wilson knocked Mr Hislop unconscious by hitting him with a lamp. Mr Hislop remained unconscious for the next 40 minutes until the ambulance crew arrived. He was not seriously injured.

While the two men were fighting, Mrs Wilson went downstairs and got a knife from the kitchen. She ran back upstairs with the knife. What happened next is not clear. She chased her husband downstairs. A few seconds later, Mrs Wilson stabbed Mr Wilson from behind in the downstairs corridor of their house. He died from a fatal wound within a few minutes.

The 5 Witnesses: Their Statements to the Police

1 Mrs Patel: Next door neighbour
She says that she heard arguments and fights quite often, and saw Mrs Wilson's bruises afterwards. She also saw Mrs Wilson's lovers coming and going. She had agreed with Mrs Wilson to keep the affairs secret. The two women were quite close friends.

2 Dr Simms: Pathologist who carried out the autopsy on Mr Wilson's body
He found two stab wounds in the back, one of which was not serious, the other was fatal. Dr Simms is not sure which wound occurred first.

3 Mr Hislop: Mrs Wilson's lover
He was only a witness to the first part of the fight and was unconscious when the stabbing occurred.

4 Mr Carmichael
Mr Wilson's colleague and good friend. He saw part of the incident through the windows of the house, although net curtains made clear vision difficult. He saw Mrs Wilson come downstairs, take the knife and go back upstairs. He also saw her chase Mr Wilson downstairs but he isn't sure if she jumped or fell on top of him just before the stabbing.

5 Mrs Wilson: The accused
She says that the stabbing was an accident and that she fell on top of her husband after running down the stairs.

You are going to role-play the trial of Mrs Wilson. Your teacher will give each of you a role to play and tell you how long you have to prepare for the trial. Decide carefully what your character would say and how he/she would act in the situation. You are free to interpret the role as you like, but make sure you don't contradict the information you are given. The witnesses must appear in the above order.

Vocabulary check

stab (v) – drive a knife or sharp object into someone or something
severely – strongly
press charges – prosecute / take to court
unconscious – like they are sleeping
fatal – causing death
wound (n) – a cut in the skin
pathologist – somebody who examines dead bodies to find out why they died
autopsy – examination of a dead body
net curtains – thin white curtains that are difficult to see through

Stabbed in the Back

Role Cards

1 Mrs Patel

You are the next-door-neighbour of the Wilson family. Mrs Wilson is your close friend, and although you never saw the fights, you often heard arguments, and saw Mrs Wilson bruised afterwards. Mrs Wilson spoke freely to you about her marriage and her affairs. She was too scared to apply for divorce. She hoped one day that she would have a lover who would be strong enough to help her get away from her husband. On several occasions she even told you that she wanted to kill him. The defending lawyers will want you to stand as a character witness for Mrs Wilson. Talk to them during the preparation time. You must decide how much of the above information to tell the court, whether you are going to hide any information, and whether you are prepared to exaggerate or even lie!

2 Dr Simms

You are the pathologist who carried out the autopsy on Mr Wilson's body. You discovered two stab wounds in the back, one of which was 6cm deep and not serious, the other was 14cm deep and directly into the heart. Death came within a few seconds. It is difficult to tell which wound happened first, although, naturally, the fact that there were two wounds makes you suspicious. Could they both have happened by accident? The murder weapon was a 20cm-long knife, but not very sharp, so it must have been driven into the back of Mr Wilson with considerable force to cause the 14cm wound. Your expert opinion will be very important to the prosecuting lawyers. Talk to them during the preparation time.

3 Mr Hislop

You met Mrs Wilson in a bar in August. Originally, you didn't know she was married. Four weeks later you found out. The 24th November was only the third time you had visited her at her house. You had arrived at the house at about 12:30, and 20 minutes or so later Mr Wilson arrived back at the house and found you half-undressed kissing his wife. He threw himself at you and a brief fight started. You suddenly lost consciousness after being hit on the head with a lamp. When you woke up there were ambulance men and policemen around you. You haven't spoken to Mrs Wilson since the incident, but you are very much in love with her. How can you exaggerate your story to help her? Are there any lies you can tell? Talk to the defending lawyers in the preparation time – Find out how you can help.

4 Mr Carmichael

You saw more of what happened than any other witness. You arrived back at the house at about 1:00pm with Mr Wilson. You waited in the car for about two minutes until you heard a scream from upstairs. You got out and ran to the door which was locked. Although net curtains made it difficult to see clearly, you could see into the kitchen and corridor reasonably well. You saw Mrs Wilson come downstairs, take the knife and go back upstairs, holding it up in front of her. One minute later you saw Mrs Wilson chase Mr Wilson downstairs. When they got to the bottom of the stairs, she seemed maybe to jump or to fall on top of him. You're not sure. The knife went into his back. As soon as she saw what she had done, Mrs Wilson was in shock, and retreated instantly from her dying husband. You are a good friend of Mr Wilson and want Mrs Wilson to go to prison. But are you prepared to lie for him? Think about it carefully and talk to the prosecuting lawyers during the preparation time.

5 Mrs Wilson

You are the only person who knows for sure whether you killed your husband on purpose! You have hated him for several years now, and often you thought about poisoning him, or causing an 'accident'. Mr Hislop is your devoted lover, but he can't help your case very well. He was unconscious when all this happened. On the 24th November, Mr Hislop arrived at about 12:30pm. You were in the bedroom with him, half-undressed and kissing when your husband arrived back. The two men started fighting and you ran downstairs to get a knife. You wanted to stop the fighting, to defend Mr Hislop. When you got back upstairs, you saw your husband hit Mr Hislop with a table lamp, knocking him unconscious. But what happened next? You decide! You know that Mr Carmichael saw you follow your husband down the stairs, but he probably couldn't have seen much detail through the net curtains, especially at the bottom of the stairs. Your best policy is to say you fell on top of him, and the knife went into his back by mistake but talk to the defending lawyers before the trial.

6 Counsel for the Defence: the defending lawyers

You know that the prosecution will prepare one of the following cases:

A Murder *To convict Mrs Wilson of murder, they must prove intent, that she wanted to kill her husband. Maximum term 25 years (life) imprisonment.*

B Manslaughter *To convict Mrs Wilson of manslaughter they must prove that she wanted to hurt him physically, but did not want to kill him. Maximum term 12 years imprisonment.*

You must be prepared to defend against either charge. Three key witnesses will be on your side – Mrs Patel, Mr Hislop and Mrs Wilson. During the preparation time find out what they know and give them advice about what to say and what not to say during the trial. Note down some key questions you are going to ask each of the five defendants during the trial. You should also be ready to give a brief opening and closing statement. Remember you have the responsibility for keeping Mrs Wilson out of prison. The teacher (or one of the students) will act as judge. S/he may disallow irrelevant questions. During the trial you can object to 'leading' questions or inaccurate speculation from the prosecuting lawyer. The judge may sustain or overrule objections. The judge can also decide on the maximum length for the questioning of each witness and for the opening and closing statements.

7 Counsel for the Prosecution: the prosecuting lawyers

You must decide which of the two following cases you are going to prepare:

A Murder *To convict Mrs Wilson of murder, you must prove intent, that she wanted to kill her husband. Maximum term 25 years (life) imprisonment.*

B Manslaughter *To convict Mrs Wilson of manslaughter you must prove that she wanted to hurt him physically, but did not want to kill him. Maximum term 12 years imprisonment.*

The Counsel for the Defence will be ready to defend against either charge. Two key witnesses will be on your side – Dr Simms and Mr Carmichael. During the preparation time find out what they know, what their honest opinions are and give them advice about what to say and what not to say during the trial. Note down some key questions you are going to ask each of the five defendants during the trial. You should also be ready to give a brief opening and closing statement. Remember you have the responsibility for putting Mrs Wilson into prison. The teacher (or one of the students) will act as judge. During the trial you can object to 'leading' questions or inaccurate speculation from the defending lawyer. The judge may sustain or overrule objections. The judge can also decide on the maximum length for the questioning of each witness and for the opening and closing statements.

8 The Judge

This role can be played by a teacher or a student. You must be in charge of the trial at all times. You may disallow irrelevant questions. You may also sustain or overrule objections. The judge can also decide on the time limits for the questioning of each witness and for the opening and closing statements. The trial must follow the pattern below:

1 Ask the prosecution 'what is the charge?' [e.g. 'We charge the defendant with murder.']
2 Ask the defendant 'How do you plead?'
3 Ask the prosecution to give their opening statement (____ minutes). [e.g. (_2_ minutes)].
4 Ask the defence to give their opening statement (____ minutes).
5 Call Mrs Patel to the witness box. Invite questions from the prosecution and then the defence (____ minutes).
6 Call Dr Simms to the witness box. Invite questions from the prosecution and then the defence (____ minutes).
7 Call Mr Hislop to the witness box. Invite questions from the prosecution and then the defence (____ minutes).
8 Call Mr Carmichael to the witness box. Invite questions from the prosecution and then the defence (____ minutes).
9 Call Mrs Wilson to the witness box. Invite questions from the prosecution and then the defence (____ minutes).
10 Ask the prosecution to give their closing statement (____ minutes).
11 Ask the defence to give their closing statement (____ minutes).
12 If there is a jury, ask them to retire to consider their verdict (____ minutes).
13 When they come back, ask them 'How do you find the defendant – guilty or not guilty?'
14 If the defendant is found not guilty she is free to leave the court. (If there is no jury, you must decide if the defendant is guilty.) If the defendant is found guilty, you must decide on the sentence: For murder the maximum term is 25 years. For manslaughter the maximum term is 12 years.

9 The Jury

You are responsible for deciding whether the defendant is guilty or not guilty. Listen carefully to the charge and the whole trial. At the end the judge will ask you to retire to consider your verdict. You must have a majority agreement to reach a verdict. If you find the defendant guilty, the judge will decide on the sentence.

Questions to discuss during the trial preparation stage:

1 What is the difference between murder and manslaughter?
2 Do you think Mrs Wilson is likely to be guilty of murder, or manslaughter?
3 Which witnesses and pieces of evidence will be most important to the trial?
4 What information will you need to know to make a definite conviction?
5 Do you expect anyone to lie in court? What signs (of lying) will you look out for?

13 Survivor: Teacher's notes

Topic focus Survival; The environment; Travel

Grammar / Functional focus Conditonal structures (1st, 2nd and 3rd conditional); Future forms (*going to* and *will*); Agreeing and disagreeing

Level / Number of students Intermediate to Advanced / Minimum three students

Time 30–40 minutes (Extension 15 minutes)

Preparation

Copy the introduction and Group discussion opposite (1 per group of 3–4 students), and the task cards (1 set per group). Cut up all sheets as indicated. Take in an image of a typical desert island to show the students during the lead-in.

1 Suggested lead-in

Write the following questions on the board for discussion in pairs: *Who was Robinson Crusoe? Where did he live? How did he get there? What problems did he face? Can you think of any similar stories of people who lived on desert islands? Could you survive alone on a desert island?* Get feedback. Students will probably know recent films such as *Castaway* and *The Beach*.

2 Introduction: Choosing three items

Put the students into teams of three to four and hand out one copy of the introduction to each team. Students read the introduction and card 1. Point out the key vocabulary beneath, which they can refer to later, and let them begin. Monitor. Even if there are two or four students in a team, make sure they understand that they have only three 'lives' per team on the island. If the team loses one or two members in the game, all the students in the class team can still take part in the decision making.

3 Continuing the "Decisions Maze"

The teams will start to ask you for card 2. Make sure they have written down their three items on their introduction sheet. Remind them to discuss all the options carefully before making any decision, then give them the card. Some teams will decide more quickly than others, so be ready with other cards. Some of the cards require them to cross items off their inventory as they use them (21 – knife; 12 – any one item; 13 – gun; 9 & 25 – food). All groups must go via three key cards: 2, 5,19. On several cards, the groups lose one member of their team (6, 20, 7, 26, 3, 13, 15, 17, 29). Obviously, if they lose all three lives, they have failed. See the maze map for more details.

4 Finishing the maze

Teams will finish at different times, and with different levels of success. To keep them busy if they finish early, get them to retrace their steps, and decide if and when they made any mistakes. They may want to try a different route!

Extension: Group discussion

Once all the teams have finished, re-group them into groups of two to four, with students from other teams. Hand out the Group discussion sheet, and let them work through the questions, comparing their experiences on the island. For higher level classes, include questions 11–14 on the sheet, which include 3rd conditional structures. For lower level classes, cut off the bottom part of the sheet as indicated. When all the groups have finished, get some general feedback, finding out how each team did. Some students might enjoy writing up an account of their adventure for homework.

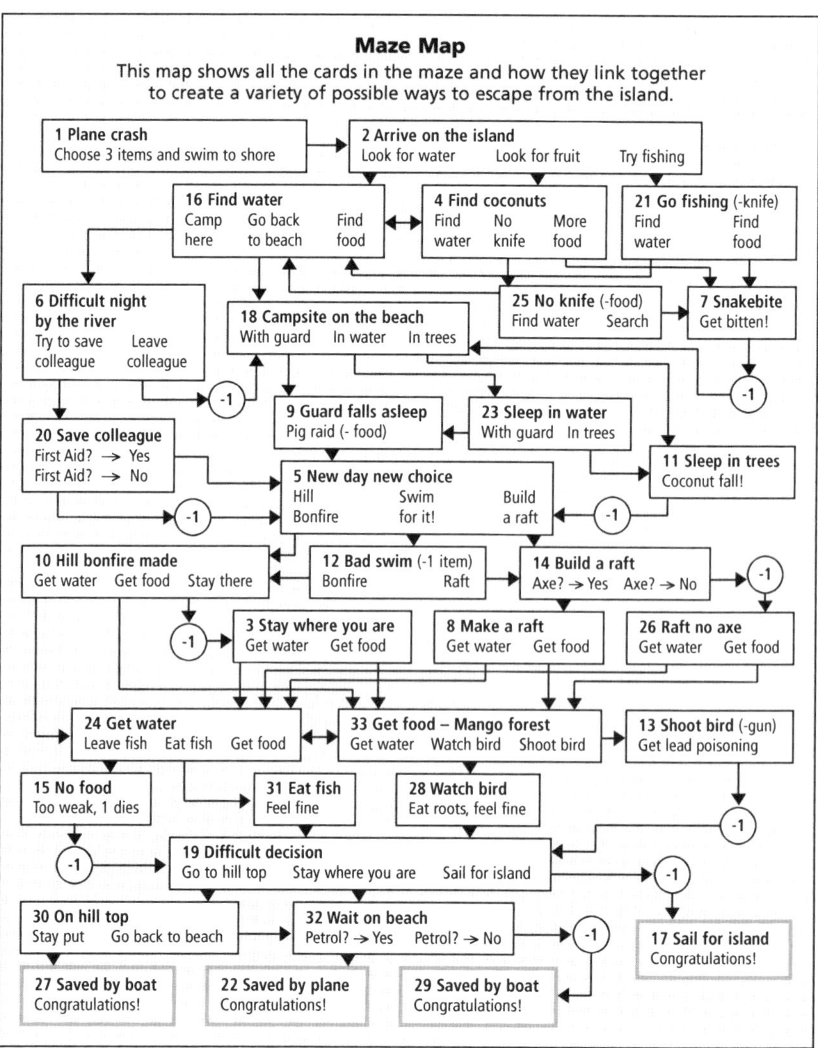

Survivor

Read card 1 below carefully. It explains the situation you are in. Your aim is to get away from the desert island safely. You will face lots of problems and dangers. At every stage, with every decision, you must think carefully if you want to survive. It won't be easy! Good luck.

1 Your plane has just crashed on a coral reef 500m from a small desert island in the Pacific Ocean. It is 3:00pm in the afternoon. There are only three of you who have survived the crash. The plane is slowly sinking under the water and you must leave it and swim to the island. One of you has a lighter, and a small waterproof moneybag to put it in. On the plane you find the following useful items:

an axe • 1 kg of airline food
a 20cm knife • a small first aid kit
1 litre of drinking water (in a plastic container)
a handgun with three bullets
1 litre of petrol (in a plastic container)

You can only take three with you to the island. You have five minutes to decide which three items you will take. Think carefully! Write the ones you decide to take here:

1) ____________________

2) ____________________

3) ____________________

Now you must swim to the shore of the island. Good luck!

Go to card 2 (ask the teacher for the card)

Key vocabulary

axe – a tool for cutting trees
bullets – the things you fire from a gun
first aid kit – important basic medical supplies
bonfire – a big fire (often to attract attention)
mango – a tropical tree with delicious fruit
exhausted – very, very tired
raft – a simple flat boat made from bits of wood
lead (n) /led/ – a metal, very poisonous
fever – serious illness with a very high temperature
dehydration – lack of water (illness)
poisonous – dangerous to eat or touch: can kill
antibiotics – medicine for serious infections
split up – divide / go off in different directions
stream – small river
container – e.g. bottle or box
shore – beach
guard / keep guard – look out for danger

Survivor

Group discussion

After you have finished the Survivor task, discuss the following questions with students from other teams:

1 Did you survive? How many of your team got away from the island? How did you get away?

2 What three things did you choose to take to the island from the plane? Why? Were they all useful?

3 If you did it again, would you choose the same things? Why (not)?

4 When you got to the beach, did you look for fruit, go fishing or look for water? What happened?

5 If you were on a real desert island, what else would you do after arriving on the island? Why?

6 On the second day, did you decide to build a raft or build a bonfire? Did it come in useful?

7 Did you come across any animals (e.g. a dead fish, a forest pig, a snake, a bird)? What happened?

9 If you really were trapped on a desert island, how would you try to find food?

10 If you had to live on a desert island for a year...
a) what book would you take with you?
b) what CD would you take with you?
c) what food would you take with you?
d) what famous person would you take with you?

11 What would you have done if you had met natives on the island?

12 How useful would these things have been on the island?
a) a fishing-line and hook
b) a mobile phone
c) a mirror
d) a botanist
e) access to the internet

13 Could you have eaten insects or worms if you had been really hungry?

14 There have been many books written and films made about survival on a desert island. Why do you think this theme is so popular? Do you think the reality would really be like the fiction?

2 You have just arrived on a beach on the island. All of you survived the swim, but you are very tired, hungry and thirsty. It is 4:30pm. It will be dark in 1½ hours.
You have three choices:

- Go into the forest to look for mangoes and coconuts among the trees: **Go to card 4**
- Try fishing next to the beach. There are lots of fish in the water: **Go to card 21**
- Go left along the beach to look for water: **Go to card 16**

What do you have with you?
What is most important to you now?

3 You stay together at the top of the hills for two hours. Unfortunately, no ships or planes are seen. What's more, there's no food or water up there. Unnoticed, one of you falls asleep with dehydration and rapidly drops into a fever. Do you have the first aid kit?

- No. You lose one team member.
- Yes. You find some aspirin and antibiotics. S/he survives.
- You must now climb down the hill, but which way?
- Climb down the hill to the stream to get some water. **Go to card 24**
- Climb down the hill towards the mango forest to look for food. **Go to card 33**

4 You have spent the last hour looking for food and you have found seven very hard coconuts, but no mangos.
Have you got the knife or the axe?

- No. **Go to card 25**
- Yes. You can open and eat the coconuts. You feel stronger.

Now what do you do?

- Go left along the beach to look for water: **Go to card 16**
- Keep looking for more food: **Go to card 7**

5 The next day is warm and sunny. You must now decide what to do. You won't survive for long on the island, so you need to be rescued within the next couple of days. You have seen one or two ships on the distant horizon already, and 20 minutes ago, a plane flew by, about five miles to the south. There is also another, larger island to the north, about three kilometres away. There is a hill in the centre of the island about 200 metres high. What would you like to do?

- Climb to the top of the hill and build a bonfire to attract attention from planes or ships. **Go to card 10**
- Go into the forest to build a raft. You could use the raft to get to the nearby island or to get closer to a passing ship. **Go to card 14**
- Try swimming to the nearby island three kilometres away. **Go to card 12**

6 There are a lot of mosquitoes and biting insects among the trees. In the middle of the night, you all wake up. One of you has a very serious fever. Is it malaria, or dehydration? You don't know. What do you do? Think carefully about what you have with you.

- Leave him/her. Try to find the way back to the beach. **Go to card 18** *(You lose one team member)*
- Stay with him/her and try to save him/her: **Go to card 20**

7 As you keep searching for food among the trees it begins to get dark. Suddenly, one of you steps on a poisonous snake and is bitten. You lose one team member! How many of you are left? Fortunately, the snake also dies, and you manage to eat it and feel a bit better. You decide to head back to the beach to sleep: **Go to card 18**

8 Using the axe, you make a good raft. It takes about two hours, but at the end you are happy with your work. Now you are both hungry and thirsty. What would you like to do?

- Go back to the stream by the beach to get some water. **Go to card 24**
- Head back towards a mango forest you found earlier to look for food. **Go to card 33**

9 Half way through the night, your guard falls asleep. Ten minutes later, s/he wakes up and notices a forest pig in the camp. If you had any food, the pig has eaten it. Cross it off your list. The pig runs away. Fortunately, the rest of the night passes without any problems. **Go to card 5**

10 The climb to the top of the hill is long and difficult. Eventually you arrive, clear a space and manage to break off enough tree branches to prepare a good bonfire. It takes you over four hours and at the end you are very tired, hungry and extremely thirsty. What do you do now?

- Climb down the hill to the stream to get some water. **Go to card 24**
- Climb down the hill towards the mango forest to look for food. **Go to card 33**
- Stay at the top of the hill, looking for ships or planes. **Go to card 3**

11 You each choose different trees to sleep in and all fall asleep. Just before dawn, one member of your team falls from a high coconut tree! The coconuts fall on top of him/her. You lose one team member, but you have a lot of coconuts for breakfast! **Go to card 5**

12 Swim for it! You set off from the beach, swimming slowly together. After about one kilometre, the sea gets quite rough and one of you gets into difficulty. You try to help, but it's no good. You lose one team member. How many of you are left? You decide to head back to shore. You arrive on the beach exhausted and must now decide what to do:

- Climb to the top of the hill and build a bonfire to attract attention from planes or ships. **Go to card 10**
- Go into the forest to build a raft. You could use the raft to get to the nearby island or to get closer to a passing ship. **Go to card 14**

(Note: you lost one of your list items on the swim. Cross it off your list.)

13 You shoot three times at the bird, using up all three bullets. It falls dead. You cook and eat it, having a really good meal. You feel much better afterwards. Then suddenly, somebody starts to vomit. It's lead poisoning, from the bullets. You lose one team member. How many of you are left? **Go to card 19**

(Cross the gun off your list)

14 You go into the forest to find some wood to make a raft. Have you got an axe?

- Yes. **Go to card 8**
- No. **Go to card 26**

15 You leave the fish and spend the next hour walking through the forest looking for food. Suddenly, one of you falls down, unconscious. Is it exhaustion or hunger? You don't know. Unfortunately, you are too weak to try to heal him / her, and you don't have any medicine with you that will help, so you lose one team member. How many of you are left? **Go to card 19**

16 After 30 minutes' walking, you have found a small stream with fresh water. You drink it and feel refreshed. But now you're very hungry, and tired. What would you like to do?

- Go and look for coconuts and mangoes among the trees: **Go to card 4**
- Stay by the river and spend the night in the forest: **Go to card 6**
- Walk all the way back to the beach and spend the night there. It will be dark by the time you get back: **Go to card 18**

17 The crossing to the nearby island is long and dangerous. Half way, your boat begins to break up, and you have to swim the rest of the way, using the pieces of wood to help you. Along the way, one of you gets into trouble and disappears beneath the water. How many of you are left?

You make it to the island, and as you come ashore, extremely tired, you notice footprints. You follow them around the island for 30 minutes, and then... amazingly you see a hotel. It's an exclusive island holiday resort. **You've survived. Congratulations!**

18 You arrive at the beach but it is completely dark. You hear strange noises coming from the bushes. Where and how would you like to sleep?

- All climb up into the trees and try to sleep there: **Go to card 11**
- Sleep on the ground, taking it in turns to guard the camp: **Go to card 9**
- Try sleeping in the warm shallow water: **Go to card 23**

What do you have with you? What could happen in the night?

19 You now have the biggest problem to solve. You are feeling very weak and tired, but you really need to keep looking for a way to get off the island. You decide to stay together for safety. You know that you will have a better chance of seeing ships or planes from the top of the hill, but there is no food or water up there. What do you do?

If you have a raft:

- You could set off for the nearby island. **Go to card 17**
- You could watch for a ship from the beach. **Go to card 32**

If you have prepared a bonfire at the top of the hill:

- You could go to the top of the hill and wait there. **Go to card 30**
- You could go back to the beach and rest, watching from there. **Go to card 32**

20 Have you got the first aid kit?

- Yes. You find antibiotics and aspirin in the kit. You give these to the sick member of the party. He/She gets better rapidly. **Go to card 5**
- No. Your colleague gets worse, and loses consciousness. How many of you are left? **Go to card 5**

21 You try fishing. Do you have the knife?

- Yes. You take it in turns to use it, but it's very difficult, and eventually one of you drops the knife under water. (Cross the knife off your list)
- No. Fishing is hopeless. Give up!

What would you like to do now?

- Try looking for food under the trees: **Go to card 7**
- Go back along the beach in search of water: **Go to card 16**

22 Thinking quickly, you pour the petrol over some bushes and small trees by the beach. Using the lighter, you set fire to the bushes. They go up in flames, and you have to run into the sea to escape the heat. Luckily, the pilot of the sea plane sees the fire and flies back to investigate. He lands and finds you tired, weak, but alive. **You've survived. Congratulations!**

23 Whose idea was this? After 20 minutes you're very cold and it's impossible to sleep. You have to go back to the beach.

- All climb up into the trees and try to sleep there: **Go to card 11**
- Sleep on the ground, taking it in turns to guard the camp: **Go to card 9**

24 You get to the stream just in time to get some water. You drink for a while, and then you notice a big dead fish floating on the surface of the water. It doesn't smell too bad, and one of you is starting to feel dizzy from hunger. What do you do?

- Cook and eat the fish: **Go to card 31**
- Leave the fish and try to survive on just water: **Go to card 15**
- Try going back to the mango forest: **Go to card 33**

25 You can't open the coconuts. You are very hungry and thirsty. Have you got food with you?

- Yes. You must use it now (cross it off the list). You now need to find water: **Go to card 16**
- No. You must keep looking for food: **Go to card 7**

26 You find it really difficult to make a raft without an axe. You have to split up to look for good wood for the raft. After one hour, you notice that somebody is missing. You go looking for him/her, but two hours later, you haven't found him/her and the raft isn't finished. You have lost him/her. How many of you are left? You finish the raft, and hope that it is strong enough. By now you are extremely hungry and thirsty. What do you do now?

- Go back to the stream by the beach to get some water. **Go to card 24**
- Head back towards a mango forest you found earlier to look for food. **Go to card 33**

27 Another two hours pass and it's starting to get dark. You're beginning to give up hope. Suddenly, from the south, you see a small ship in the distance. You light the bonfire on the top of the hill. It takes some time, but it shows up well in the night sky. The boat starts to move towards the island. They've seen you. 1 hour later, you've been rescued by the crew of a ship from New Zealand. **You've survived. Congratulations!**

28 After watching the bird for ten minutes, you notice it's eating the roots from a green ground plant. You pull up one or two of these plants, and the roots look like potatoes. You are so hungry that you have to eat them. Luckily, they are tasty and not poisonous. You feel much better and relax for a while in the sun. **Go to card 19**

29 Unfortunately, not having any petrol, you can't start a fire quickly enough to attract the attention of the pilot. So you run out into the water, waving your arms and shouting. The pilot doesn't see you, and the plane disappears towards the horizon.

You spend another terrible night on the beach. The next morning, you are woken up by the sound of a motorboat. Local fishermen are arriving on the island. You jump up for joy, only to notice that one member of your party has not survived the night. **Other members of your party have all survived. Congratulations!**

30 You get to the top of the hill. You wait up there for two hours and start to feel tired. What do you do?

- Stay at the top of the hill: **Go to card 27**
- Go back down to the beach to rest. **Go to card 32**

31 You cook the fish well and eat it. Ten minutes later, you all begin to feel a bit sick. Fortunately, it's nothing serious, perhaps not enough food. You rest for another half hour and feel much better and stronger. **Go to card 19**

32 The day passes as you wait on the beach. Too tired to look for food, you stay there, hoping to be saved. Suddenly, just as it's getting darker you hear the sound of a small sea plane passing overhead. Quick, you need to do something. Have you got the petrol?

- Yes. **Quick, go to card 22**
- No. **Quick, go to card 29**

33 You get to the mango forest. Unfortunately, the mangoes aren't in season, and you can't find any fruit. Then suddenly, you see a big bird looking for food on the ground.

- If you've got a gun, you could try shooting it. If you want to shoot it, **go to card 13.**
- Stay in the mango forest with the bird: **Go to card 28**
- Head down to the stream to get some water: **Go to card 24**

14 Front Page News: Teacher's notes

Topic focus Newspapers; Journalism; Football and sport; Flying and airports

Grammar / Functional focus Question forms; Reported speech; Tabloid newspaper register

Level / Number of students Intermediate to Advanced / Minimum six students

Time 60–75 minutes (Extension 15 minutes)

Preparation

Copy the main synopsis sheet and the additional information (one copy of each per group of 3–4 students). Cut up as indicated. Take to the lesson: One blank sheet of A3 paper per group, two black marker pens, a pair of scissors and a glue pen. If you can, try to find another teacher who will play the role of the other main character during the interviews (*see below*).

1 Suggested lead-in

Pre-teach: *tabloid (newspaper)* Elicit the names of five national newspapers and write them on the board with the following questions for discussion in pairs (5 mins): *Which paper would you buy if you needed information about... politics / sport / celebrity gossip / business and finance? Which newspapers... are more serious / are more fun to read / are more reliable / have more pictures?*

2 Creating the teams of journalists

Put the students into groups of 3–4. Tell them that today they are a team of tabloid journalists, and that they are going to write a story for the front page of their newspaper. Ask them to think of a name for their newspaper and to decide on the following roles: editor, reporter(s), writer(s).

3 The synopsis – Breaking news

Hand out the synopsis sheet (1 per group) and read through it with them. Give them five minutes to prepare questions for the interview. Monitor and help if necessary.

4 Selecting the two main characters

You, the teacher, can play one of the two roles at the airport interviews. [male teachers – Michael Waters, female teachers – Susan McGee]. The other role could be played by another teacher or a student in class. These roles are best played by teachers, who can improvise more freely and provide stimulating and realistic characters. If you use a student, take them from their team as soon as the preparation for the interviews starts (choose a writer or an editor) and provide assistance where necessary. The two role-players should read the role-play cards carefully, and think about what they are going to say, do etc. during the interviews.

5 Interviews with the Press

Put a chair in the middle of the room. Emphasise that they have only five minutes for each interview. Tell the reporters to ask the questions and the writers to take notes / quotes. Start with Michael Waters. The interviewees can improvise on the role if necessary.

6 Writing the stories

Now give the tabloid teams a deadline for when the stories must be finished (25–40 minutes). Hand out a front page (sheet of A3 paper) to each group and show them the stationery for when they need to add headlines, pictures, etc. If you have recently studied reported speech, encourage them to use it in their articles (*also see Extension below*).

7 Additional information – Stop Press!

Give out a new piece of information (photos, quotes, facts) to each group every few minutes during the writing phase. The editor should choose what to include or reject. Make sure that you have given out all the information at least ten minutes before the deadline.

8 Reading the front pages

When they finish, put the stories up on the classroom walls, and let each team go round and read the front pages of the other newspapers 'hot off the press'!

9 Group discussion

Re-group the students from different newspapers together and write the following questions on the board for a five-minute discussion: *Which of the papers seems to be more factual? Which is more tabloid? Which would you buy? How did you choose your headline and pictures? Was it difficult to get the story written in time? Are all your facts accurate?*

Extension – What they said (Reported speech)

Put the students into pairs or threes and hand out the sheet. Read through the instructions and give them five to ten minutes to convert the direct speech into reported speech. Check the answers.

Answers

2 Michael Waters' wife said that he had been a terrible husband and that he would probably get married again and ruin someone else's life. **3** Southtown United confirmed that Michael Waters would be playing in Saturday's match, unless he was in prison! **4** Michael Waters claimed that Susan was just another pretty woman who was in love with him and that this kind of thing happened to him every day. **5** Susan explained that she hadn't wanted to kiss him, but that he had insisted. She also said that's when she had spilt the champagne on him. **6** The paparazzi photographer told us that he could sell us a secret photograph that he had taken during the flight, and asked us if we wanted to buy it. **7** One of the other passengers said that he had seen Michael Waters and the flight attendant and that they had been kissing for a long time.

Front Page News

Work in groups of three to four.

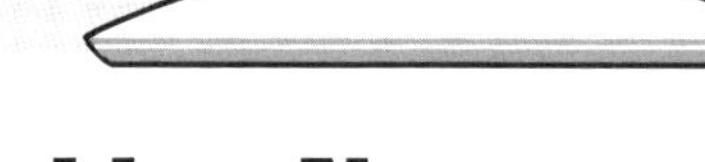

You are a team of reporters and journalists who work for a tabloid newspaper. Think of a name for your newspaper.

Now read this!

Breaking News...

A football player has been arrested for causing a fight on a plane. The British Airways plane landed at Heathrow Airport 30 minutes ago. The player is still being interviewed by the police there. It is believed to be a famous Southtown United player. There is a rumour that an attractive female flight attendant was also involved. Get to the airport quickly and try to get interviews with the football player and also the flight attendant as they leave the airport! I'm counting on you guys to put together a great front page story!

Good luck,

Ian, Chief Editor

You have five minutes until the interview. Think carefully about what questions the reporter is going to ask. What details do you want to know? Do you need any quotes? Who is going to ask the questions and who is going to record the answers?

When you get back from the airport, you should write an article for the newspaper, working together. Your teacher will tell you how much time you have. You need to think of a good headline for the article.

You will also receive other information throughout the 'day', such as statements from other people, photographs and facts. So be aware! Try to add the new information as you go along to make the most interesting article. It won't be easy, but it's all in a day's work for a newspaper journalist!

Vocabulary check

tabloid newspaper – a daily newspaper that is mainly interested in gossip rather than serious news
rumour – an unconfirmed story or report
count on – depend on (at an important time)
quote (n) – the exact words that somebody said (always in quotation marks: " ")
headline – the title of a newspaper article
statement – a specially prepared speech, given to journalists

Front Page News – Additional Information

Role Card: The football player Michael Waters (Southtown United)

You are drunk. You were on a plane a few hours ago, and had too many drinks. A beautiful flight attendant was pouring you some champagne and you wanted to whisper something in her ear. **[You decide what you said]** Then she poured the champagne over you and slapped you in the face. You swore at her and stood up. Another male flight attendant ran up to you and you punched him. **[Decide what you are going to tell the newspapers when you come out of the airport!]** Remember that you are married, and that you could lose your job if you say the wrong thing. But also remember that there were plenty of other people on the plane who may have seen what happened.

whisper – say something quietly
swore (swear) – say bad or rude words
punch – hit with your hand, like a boxer

Role Card: The airline flight attendant Susan McGee

You are a beautiful young flight attendant for British Airways. Michael Waters, the famous footballer, was on your plane. You were serving him some champagne when he grabbed hold of you, pulled you down and tried to kiss you. By mistake you poured the champagne over him. He got extremely angry, started swearing and tried to hit you, but you ran away. Another steward came to help you and Mr Waters hit him as well. You are very upset, because he is your favourite football player and you don't want him to get into trouble.

swear – say bad or rude words

Susan McGee

You have just received the following statement from Southtown United:

"Michael Waters is a great player and the club fully supports him. As far as we know, he gave up drinking six months ago after we advised him to stop. He is currently going through some difficulties in his marriage at the moment."

Statement from Waters' wife

"I have filed for divorce. He was too violent in our marriage. I have no sympathy for him. I'm just surprised that this never happened before. He was always doing similar things to me!"

file for divorce – ask for an end to a marriage (formal English)
sympathy – feeling sorry for someone

Anonymous statement from a passenger on the plane

"From where I was sitting, Mr Waters and the flight attendant were kissing for about 20 seconds. She got so excited that she forgot about the champagne and poured it onto him by mistake."
This quote could be unreliable.

Background research information

It has been found out that Susan McGee was a glamour model and that she has also had flings with three other famous footballers.

glamour model – a model who does topless and nearly naked photos
fling – short love affair

One of your journalists has found out the following information:

The British Airways flight was from New York to London and arrived at 11:10am. Waters had been in New York with his wife, but they had an argument of some kind and he left without her.

Paparazzi Photo

A member of the paparazzi has offered you this photo for £3000. He says it was taken during the flight. Do you want to buy it?

paparazzi – private photographers who work like detectives, photographing the rich and famous

Archive Photo

One of your journalists has found the following photo of Michael Waters.

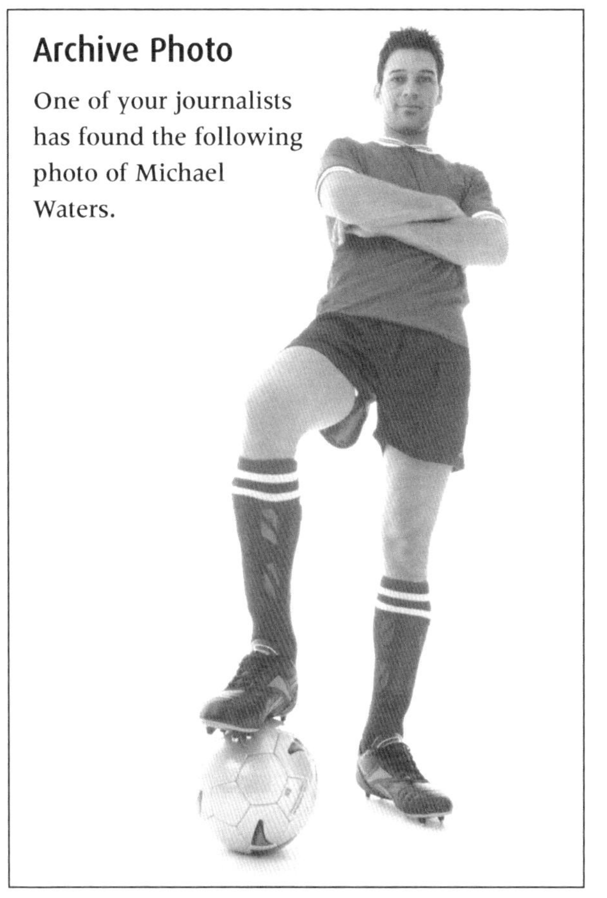

Front Page News

What They Said

Look at the following quotations. They all come from the tabloid news story that you wrote. Decide who probably said them and rewrite them using reported speech and an appropriate reporting verb.

e.g. **1** One of the other flight attendants said that Mr Waters had been attacking Susan and that he had run to help her.

1 Mr Waters was attacking Susan. Naturally, I ran to help her.

2 He's been a terrible husband. He'll probably get married again and ruin someone else's life.

3 Michael Waters will be playing in Saturday's match... unless he is in prison!

4 She's just another pretty woman who is in love with me. This kind of thing happens to me every day.

5 I didn't want to kiss him, but he insisted. That's when I spilt the champagne.

6 I can sell you a secret photograph that I took during the flight. Do you want to buy it?

7 I saw Michael Waters and the flight attendant. They were kissing for a long time.

15 Hungry For Haiku: Teacher's notes

Topic focus Poetry; Places / Geography; Rhythm in language

Grammar / Functional focus Describing places, things, people; Word order in sentences

Level / Number of students Upper intermediate to Advanced / Minimum two students

Time 40–50 minutes (Extension 20 minutes extra)

Preparation

Copy the worksheet opposite (1 per student) and the haiku cards (1 copy of each haiku per group). Cut up the cards as indicated.

1 Suggested lead-in

Write the following questions on the board for discussion in groups of three to four (5 mins): *Do you often read poetry? What kind of poetry do you like? Have you ever written any poetry? What about? When? Why? Do you think poems have to rhyme to be good?*

2 Reading a haiku

Introduce the theme of haiku and find out what the students know about it. Hand out the worksheets and let them read the poem and go through the questions in their groups. Listen carefully and help with pronunciation and rhythm. Get feedback at the end.

3 Syllable analysis

Read through part 2 for them and let them count the number of syllables in each line.

Answer
1st line: 5 syllables; 2nd line: 7 syllables; 3rd line: 5 syllables

Note: *Nearly all haiku follows this pattern, but there are exceptions, especially in translation.*

4 Haiku cards

Shuffle and hand out the haiku cards for the first poem, one set for each group. Students put it together (5 mins). Monitor carefully, helping with grammar and vocabulary. Remind them to count the syllables in each line. As they finish, move them on to the discussion questions. Get feedback to compare impressions. Repeat with one of the other three poems. Choose the poem you think will appeal most to your class. The original haikus are given on the haiku card pages.

Note: *Students may find other grammatically possible solutions for the haiku. Don't forget to praise any alternative solutions that are acceptable grammatically.*

5 Haiku composition

Tell the students that they are now going to write a haiku. Each group should agree on one of the themes from the worksheet, and then they should work alone in silence for two or three minutes to write down some words. Working alone, they are likely to come up with a greater variety of ideas. Monitor discreetly.

Tip: *If you think it will help, put on some ambient background music while they are thinking.*

After three minutes, tell them to work in groups again. Give them ten minutes to finish their haiku. Monitor actively, providing suggestions and approval.

6 Haiku presentation

Ask one member of each group to come to the front of the class and read out their haiku. Alternatively, in a big class, you could get them to mix and mingle, reading out their haiku on a one-to-one basis.

Extension – Classroom posters

If the students have enjoyed creating the haiku, why not encourage them to make haiku posters to put on the classroom wall? They can find images in magazines to glue onto their posters, draw their own illustrations, etc.

Students could also try writing another haiku for homework. They could use one of the suggested themes or think of their own.

Extra Information on haiku
True haiku also has one other characteristic not mentioned above: no metaphors or similes are ever used, to ensure that the image created is direct and instant. Your students might be interested to know this, and may find examples of (inappropriately used) metaphor in the haiku they have studied in this lesson. e.g. in haiku 1, 'I heard someone die' could be considered a metaphor, as the death was not heard in any literal sense.

Hungry For Haiku

Work in groups of three to four.

1 Have a look at this poem:

Took the last bus home
Four wheels for sleepy bodies
Our eyes met just once.

- What is it about?
- What images do you see when you read it?
- How does it make you feel?
- Do you like it?
- Read it out. Try to get the correct rhythm of the poem.

2 **The poem is an example of 'haiku', a Japanese form of poetry that has only three short lines. A haiku is an attempt to create a 'photograph' in words. In the three lines there are usually only 17 syllables.**

- Look at the poem again. How many syllables are there in each line?

3 **Your teacher will now give you the words to some other haiku poems.**

Work in teams to order the words into a haiku. Remember how many syllables there must be in each line and try to create a poem that sounds good when you read it. There may be more than one possible solution to each haiku. After you complete each one, the teacher will tell you the original haiku. Discuss the same questions after each one:

- What is it about?
- What images do you see when you read it?
- How does it make you feel?
- Do you like it?
- Read it out. Try to get the correct rhythm of the poem.

4 **Now it's time for you to try writing your own haiku.**

Choose one of the following themes:

Life in the city
Morning in winter
The airport
Man and animals
A mysterious bookshop
An old church
Football

Note down five to ten words that come into your head when you think of the theme.

Work together in your groups to put your ideas together and write your own haiku!

5 **When you have finished, read your haiku out to the class.**

Haiku 1

The dripping tap slowed
Just then before the phone rang
I heard someone die

tap	just	the	slowed
dripping	phone	someone	die
then	I	rang	before
the	heard		

Haiku 2

Alone I cling to
The freezing mountain and see
White cloud below me.

to	cloud	freezing	see
me	alone	cling	the
and	white	below	I
mountain			

Haiku 3

His postcard was lost
Words that India inspired
Were absorbed and found

India	were	and	was
that	absorbed	found	postcard
inspired	lost	his	words

Haiku 4

All done without thought
Dogs taste blood. A fox is caught.
And they call it sport?

taste	done	thought	is
call	a	without	dogs
fox	caught	it	all
they	sport	blood	and

16 Great Inventions: Teacher's notes

Topic focus Inventions; Communication; Science; Technology; Media

Grammar / Functional focus Passive voice; Superlative adjectives; Infinitive of purpose

Level / Number of students Intermediate to Advanced / Minimum six students

Time 40–60 minutes (Extension 15–20 minutes; Family Fortunes 30 minutes)

Preparation

Copy the three texts (1 per student). If you are going to use the extension make one copy per three to four students.

1 Suggested lead-in

Write the following question on the board for discussion in pairs (5 mins): *What new inventions have changed our way of life in the 20th century? Think about... transport, communications, entertainment, food and cooking, work*

2 First reading in original groups

Divide the class into three groups of equal numbers. Give out text A to the students in one group, text B to the second group and text C to the third group. Students read the text (4–6 mins.). Optional global reading task: *How many people contributed to the invention? Who was the most important?* Monitor carefully. Difficult words are underlined and explained in the vocabulary check.

3 Jigsaw exchange stage

Re-organise the groups so that each new group includes at least one student who has read each of the three texts. Students ask each other the key questions (which are the same for all three texts) in their new groups. Each student should answer for the invention that they have read about, explaining vocabulary if needed. Monitor. As each group finishes, move them on to the discussion questions.

Answers

Text A 1 In the 1960s **2** The US government intended to use it to link up computers in research institutes / universities. **3** Data is transferred through telephone lines in 'packaged' groups which are read by modem. Information is accessed via a special programme (browser). **4** The first problem was to improve data transfer; done through packaging groups of data together. The other problem mentioned was to do with software. The first user-friendly browser, 'Mosaic' was developed by Andreessen and co. **5** Other dates: 1972 – development of e-mail; 1989 – introduction of World-Wide Web and html. Names: Frank Heart who oversaw development of hardware (e.g. modem).
Text B 1 In 1947. **2** For police car radios in USA. **3** Cell phones are like two-way radios, communicating over long distances through countrywide transmitters, each with its own 'cell'. **4** Usage was a major problem. Due to radio wavelengths being limited, there is only room for a limited number of calls in each cell. The US government helped (1968) – it allowed a wider range of radio wavelengths for mobile calls. The mobility problem was solved by Martin Cooper who developed the portable mobile phone (1973). The final hurdle was getting government approval for a nationwide network which was granted (1982).
5 Other dates: 1978 – first trials of the network. Organisations: Bell Laboratories – developed the first police mobile phones. Richard Dronsuth and Albert Mikulski – two of eight Bell inventors; Motorola – Bell's rivals. Cooper worked for Motorola.
Text C 1 In 1843. **2** To send simple written messages down a telegraph line. **3** The page is divided into thin lines. Each line is then broken up into black and white dots and sent down the telegraph line as electronic signals. Signals are put together at the other end. **4** The first problem: Bain's fax was usurped by telephones, which sent simple messages more efficiently. In 1865, pantélégraph was an improvement, but still couldn't send useful images e.g. photos. Arthur Korn solved this problem in 1902 – he invented 'telephotography', a primitive means of scanning and transmitting images. The final improvement was to make them smaller, more practical and compatible with standard telephone lines: Rank Xerox did this in 1966. **5** By 1907 photos for newspapers were being sent along telephone lines.

4 Class feedback

Having completed the key questions and the discussion stage, get feedback on difficult / interesting answers as a class.

Extension: Great Inventions – But When?

Preparation

Copy and cut up the Great Inventions... But When? worksheet (one per group of three to four students).

Method

Divide the class into groups of three to four students. Hand out the worksheet and read through the instructions with them. They should agree before they write a date. If you have been studying the passive recently, ask them: *Which of the sentences are passive?* (All of them) *Which tense?* (Past simple passive) *Why is the passive voice used in these sentences?* (To focus attention more on the invention than the inventor [the agent]).

Answers

1925 TV; 1866 Dynamite; 1827 Typewriter;
1939 Helicopter; 1913 Bra; 1858 Washing-machine;
1985 Windows; 1880 Toilet paper; 1799 Battery;
1968 Mouse; 1902 Lie detector

Extra Idea: *Students turn over / cover their worksheet. Ask them: What happened in 1913? etc. They must answer in the passive.*

Great Inventions

Text A

The Internet

Already it seems difficult to imagine a world without the internet or e-mail. We use it for communicating with family, friends and colleagues, for getting news and information, and even for shopping. But when exactly did it start, and where did it come from?

The internet was first thought of in the 1960s by a US government agency (the ARPA) as a way to link computers in universities and research centres across the USA. The first major problem the project faced was to improve the efficiency of data transfer over telephone lines. Fortunately, in 1962, Leonard Kleinrock, then a student, invented a special technology that greatly increased the speed of data transfer by packaging groups of data together. This allowed computers to communicate with each other freely and quickly.

The necessary hardware for the network was designed by scientists under the supervision of Frank Heart and the network was ready for use in September 1969. Although it was slow to start with, the network was an immediate success. It grew quickly, and in 1972 Ray Tomlinson introduced electronic mail (e-mail) to the system. By the late 1980s, many other organisations and companies wanted to use a similar communication system, and the term 'internet' came into use. In 1989, Tim Berners-Lee proposed the idea of a World-Wide Web project (www) and a new universal language called HTML.

The final problem to be solved was in the software department. For the internet to become accessible to the general public, a simple interface needed to be created. And, in 1991, a group of students at the University of Illinois, led by 21-year-old Marc Andreessen developed the first 'browser' programme called Mosaic. In keeping with the ideals of the internet, Mosaic was free! Netscape and Microsoft Explorer soon followed and the internet as we know it today was born.

Vocabulary check

efficiency – how well something works
data transfer – moving data from one computer to another
packaging – putting together
hardware – the different physical or permanent parts of a computer
supervision – guidance, management
proposed – suggested
software – programmes to use on a computer
interface – a means of communicating with a computer

Key questions

1. When did development first begin?
2. What was the original use for the invention?
3. How does the technology work?
4. What problems were encountered? How were they solved?
5. What other dates, names and organisations are mentioned? Why are they significant?

Discussion

1. Which of the 3 inventions...
   a) was the most amazing? Why?
   b) had the most difficult problems to solve?
   c) has had the largest influence over the 20th century? How?
   d) will be most important for the 21st century? In what way?
2. How do you think communication will change and develop over the 21st century?
3. What advantages will this bring to our way of life?
4. Could it bring any problems?

Great Inventions

Text B

Mobile Phones

With over 388 million users in Europe alone, the mobile phone industry has grown beyond all belief in less than 20 years. For many of us, life without them would be almost impossible. But what are the origins of the mobile phone?

The basic technology for mobile phones was developed in 1947 by a team of eight scientists including Richard Dronsuth and Albert Mikulski at Bell Laboratories in the USA. The phones were designed for police cars and the technology was simple. Mobile (or cell) phones are two-way radios, transmitting on the same wavelength over a short distance. To increase the distance, local transmitters that can send and receive signals over a small area (called a cell) are used. But despite the success of the police radio, it was a lot more difficult to make this technology available to the general public.

The first problem was with usage. Radio wavelengths are limited. If everybody is sending and receiving signals, the wavelengths get too busy. The US government only allowed companies to use a few limited wavelengths. It was only in 1968 that the government finally agreed to make more radio waves available to encourage the development of mobile phone technology. The second problem was with mobility. Bell Laboratory phones were still too big to be mobile, except in a car. Then, in 1973, Dr Martin Cooper at Motorola invented the first mobile handset. And his first phone call was to his rivals at Bell Laboratories!

In 1978, the first cell phone trials were carried out in Chicago, followed a year later by similar trials in Tokyo. The industry didn't really take off in the USA until 1982, when the government finally allowed widespread commercial use of mobile phones. With further technological advances in the late 1980s, mobile phones became more efficient and cheaper, and cellular networks began to develop all over the world.

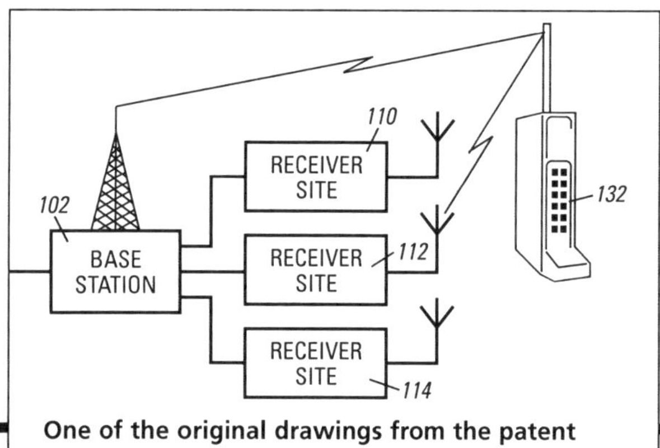

One of the original drawings from the patent for the first mobile phone

Vocabulary check

designed – put ideas into pictures and plans
transmitting – sending radio messages (*transmitter* – radio tower)
wavelength – radio messages or signals are sent in waves (e.g. short wave / long wave)
usage – how something is used
signal (*n*) – the smallest part of a complete radio message
encourage – stimulate, help to develop
handset – the part of a phone that you hold
trials – tests (*carry out trials* – do tests)
take off – (*here*) increase suddenly
efficient – good at working, useful

Key questions

1 When did development first begin?
2 What was the original use for the invention?
3 How does the technology work?
4 What problems were encountered? How were they solved?
5 What other dates, names and organisations are mentioned? Why are they significant?

Discussion

1 Which of the 3 inventions...
   a) was the most amazing? Why?
   b) had the most difficult problems to solve?
   c) has had the largest influence over the 20th century? How?
   d) will be most important for the 21st century? In what way?
2 How do you think communication will change and develop over the 21st century?
3 What advantages will this bring to our way of life?
4 Could it bring any problems?

Great Inventions

Text C

The Fax Machine

Even today, in the age of internet communications, over 400 million documents and images are sent by fax every day. It's easy, cheap and quick to send a fax. But the fax machine itself is far older than many of us may think...

Incredibly, the fax machine was invented in 1843, 33 years before the telephone! The inventor was a Scotsman, Alexander Bain, who also invented the first electric clock.

The idea behind his fax machine was very simple, and has hardly changed over the last 150 years. The page is divided into thin lines. Each line is then broken up into black and white dots and sent down a telegraph line as electronic signals. These signals are then put together at the other end. Unfortunately, Bain's machine was only able to send simple messages, and telephones were soon to become far better at doing this.

By 1865, the first commercial faxes were being sent in France, called 'pantélégraphes', but the main problem with these early faxes was that the technology was too simple to send useful images, such as photographs. This all changed in 1902, when Arthur Korn invented 'telephotography', a way of scanning and transmitting photographs. By 1907 photos for newspapers were being sent along telephone lines.

But, for the next 60 years, as millions of telephones were installed into offices and houses, only a few fax machines existed worldwide. They were too big, too difficult to use, and needed special phone systems. Then, in 1966 the Xerox company introduced a new 17kg fax machine that could use any telephone line to transmit fax messages. From this moment, sales of fax machines took off and they became smaller, cheaper and started a revolution in business document communication.

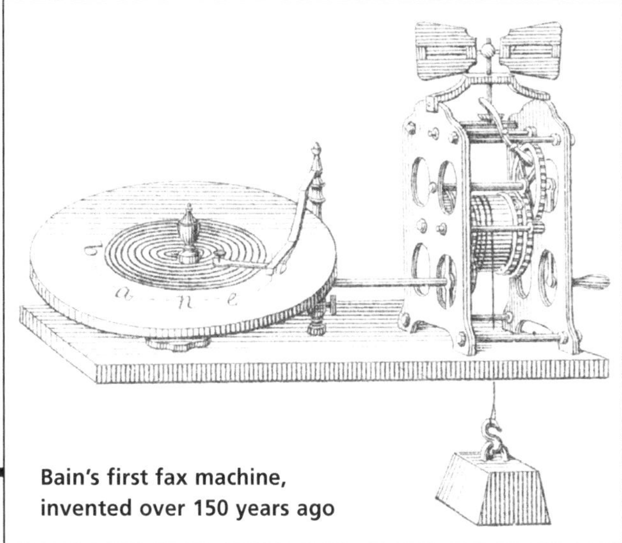

Bain's first fax machine, invented over 150 years ago

Vocabulary check

incredibly – amazingly (difficult to believe)
hardly – very little / almost nothing
divided – broken up
dots – tiny marks
signals – many electronic signals make up a whole message
scanning – reading an image with light
transmitting – sending messages (as radio or electronic signals)
installed into – put into
took off – (*here*) increased

Key questions

1 When did development first begin?
2 What was the original use for the invention?
3 How does the technology work?
4 What problems were encountered? How were they solved?
5 What other dates, names and organisations are mentioned? Why are they significant?

Discussion

1 Which of the 3 inventions...
   a) was the most amazing? Why?
   b) had the most difficult problems to solve?
   c) has had the largest influence over the 20th century? How?
   d) will be most important for the 21st century? In what way?
2 How do you think communication will change and develop over the 21st century?
3 What advantages will this bring to our way of life?
4 Could it bring any problems?

Great Inventions... But When?

Working in teams, discuss when each of the inventions listed below could have been invented. Write one of the dates in the box next to each invention. Your teacher will tell you the correct answers after you have finished.

1799 • 1827 • 1858 • 1866 • 1880 • 1902 • 1913 • 1925 • 1939 • 1968 • 1985

- [ ] The first TV picture was transmitted by John Logie Baird.
- [ ] The first dynamite was tested by Alfred Nobel.
- [ ] The first letter was typed on a typewriter by W. A. Burt.
- [ ] The first helicopter was flown successfully under the supervision of Igor Sikorsky.
- [ ] The first bra was worn by Mary Phelps Jacob.
- [ ] The first clothes were washed in a rotary washing machine by Hamilton Smith.
- [ ] The Windows program was invented by Microsoft.
- [ ] The first toilet paper was sold by the British Perforated Paper Company.
- [ ] The first battery was invented by Count Alessandro Volta.
- [ ] The computer mouse was invented by Douglas Engelbart.
- [ ] The first Lie Detector or Polygraph Machine was tried out by James Mackenzie.

Great Inventions... But When?

Working in teams, discuss when each of the inventions listed below could have been invented. Write one of the dates in the box next to each invention. Your teacher will tell you the correct answers after you have finished.

1799 • 1827 • 1858 • 1866 • 1880 • 1902 • 1913 • 1925 • 1939 • 1968 • 1985

- [ ] The first TV picture was transmitted by John Logie Baird.
- [ ] The first dynamite was tested by Alfred Nobel.
- [ ] The first letter was typed on a typewriter by W. A. Burt.
- [ ] The first helicopter was flown successfully under the supervision of Igor Sikorsky.
- [ ] The first bra was worn by Mary Phelps Jacob.
- [ ] The first clothes were washed in a rotary washing machine by Hamilton Smith.
- [ ] The Windows program was invented by Microsoft.
- [ ] The first toilet paper was sold by the British Perforated Paper Company.
- [ ] The first battery was invented by Count Alessandro Volta.
- [ ] The computer mouse was invented by Douglas Engelbart.
- [ ] The first Lie Detector or Polygraph Machine was tried out by James Mackenzie.

Great Inventions: Family Fortunes

Preparation

None, although you could find some TV game show props (e.g. microphone, question cards).

Procedure

1 The teams

Divide the students into two 'families' and tell them that they are going to play a popular TV game show called family fortunes. Draw two points columns on the board. Tell them that 100 people were asked three questions on inventions and science, and that they have to guess the most popular answers in the survey. For each question the teams must nominate a student to come to the front of the class.

2 Gaining control

Stand the two nominees facing each other and read out question 1:

> *We asked 100 Americans: What is the greatest invention of the 20th century? What were the most popular answers?*

Accept the first answer and say:

> *Okay, (student 1), you said that the greatest invention of the 20th century was __________, our survey said it was...*

If the answer is on the list below, tell them which position it was in and write it in their column, giving them the % as points (e.g. 10 points for Television, 13 for Electricity, etc.) If the answer isn't on the list, say our survey said it was not given. Obviously, if student 1 gave the most popular answer, s/he gets control of the question. If not, ask the second student to think of a more popular answer. Give student 2 a few seconds and say:

> *Okay, (student 2), you said that the greatest invention of the 20th century was __________, our survey said it was...*

The student who gave the most popular answer gets control of the question and can confer with his / her team. They can choose to play or pass. If they play, they must guess enough of the answers correctly to score at least 50 points. If they pass, the other team must score at least 50 points.

3 Team A plays (trying to score the points)

Tell the team that is playing that there are nine answers to get. Ask them for another answer, warning them that three wrong answers will give control over to the other team. Keep going, repeating the key phrases and scoring on the board until either they score 50 points, in which case they get to keep the points, or until they have given three wrong answers. If the latter happens, pass control over to the other team.

4 Team B plays (trying to steal the points)

When control goes over to the other team, tell them they have one chance to guess one of the remaining answers. Give them 30 seconds to confer. Give them all the points if they guess successfully, plus the points for their answer. If their answer is not listed, team A get to keep the points.

5 Rounds 2 & 3

Repeat the whole procedure with the other three questions below, starting with nominees at the front. The team with the most points at the end of the 'show' are the winners.

Extra Idea: *If your students enjoyed the game, try to find more questions – look on the internet – searching for 'survey', 'most popular', 'percent', etc. and play it regularly.*

1 We asked 100 Americans: 'What is the greatest invention of the 20th century?' What were the most popular answers?

Response	%
1 Computers / the Internet	21
2 Automobile (car)	15
3 Electricity	13
4 Television	10
5 Telephone / Telecommunications	9
6 Aeroplane	7
7 New medicines / vaccinations	5
8 Credit Cards	4
9 The Cinema	3

2 We asked 100 British people: 'What is your least favourite invention?' What were the most popular answers?

Response	%
1 Atomic / Nuclear weapons	31
2 Landmines	22
3 (Internal combustion) Engine	11
4 Plastic Bags	8
5 Speed Cameras	8
6 Mobile Phones	7
7 Car alarms	6
8 Television	4
9 Sinclair C5 (electric car)	2
10 Milk cartons	2

3 In 1995, we asked 100 Americans: 'Which invention would you find it most difficult to live without?' What were the most popular answers?

Response	%
1 The automobile (car)	24
2 The lightbulb	21
3 The telephone	15
4 The television	12
5 Aspirin / Paracetamol	11
6 The microwave oven	5
7 The computer	5

17 Natural Born Killers: Teacher's notes

Topic focus Animals; Nature; The environment

Grammar / Functional focus Superlatives; Asking questions; Giving advice; Reporting statistics

Level / Number of students Upper intermediate to Advanced / Minimum four students

Time 40–50 minutes (Extension 15 minutes)

Preparation

Copy the four Animal Fact Files (2 per team of two to four students) and the Amazing Animals Quiz (1 per team). Take some photos of dangerous animals to class if possible.

1 Suggested lead-in

Tell the students to write down ten animals that are dangerous to people (1 min). Get feedback on the board and add the following questions for discussion in pairs: *Which is the most dangerous? Why? Which do you most fear?*

2 Devising the questions

Put the students into four groups of equal size (ideally two to four in each group). If you have over 16 students, divide the class in two. Tell them that they are going to meet a team of experts on the following four 'dangerous animals': sharks, snakes, bears, and tigers. Tell each group to write down three questions they would like to ask about each animal. Put examples on the board: *What is the biggest shark in the world? What should you do if you are bitten by a snake?* Monitor.

Suggestion: *If you have studied superlatives or language for giving advice recently, encourage the students to incorporate this into their questions.*

3 Reading the fact files

Hand out a different fact file to each group. Give them ten minutes to read the fact file and to try to find the answers to their own questions about this animal. Difficult vocabulary is underlined and explained in the vocabulary check.

4 Presentations: Asking the experts

Now it's time for them to take the role of the experts. Put some chairs at the front of the classroom and introduce Group A as 'world famous experts on sharks'. The other three groups now ask the questions they wrote earlier about sharks. Encourage follow-up questions and ask a few yourself to elicit other interesting facts. Make a note of any unanswered questions (see: **6 Homework** idea). Continue in this way until all four groups have played the role of experts.

5 Round up: discussion

Re-group the students with one of each expert in each new group. Put these discussion questions on the board (5–8 mins): *1) Which of the animals is the most dangerous to man? 2) Which are in danger from man? How? 3) Are you still scared of any of these animals? Why? 4) Do you think it's important to protect these animals? Why? 5) What would the world be like without them?*

Extension: Amazing Animals Quiz

Hand out the quiz to each group and give them ten minutes to decide which are true or false. Encourage them to discuss their decisions. Check the answers at the end. There is some extra information below that the students will probably be interested in.

Answers

1T Swifts soar up to high altitude and glide in the air for short periods, sleeping as they do. Swifts also mate, drink and collect nesting material in the air. If they land on the ground, they have difficulty taking off again.

2T Royal jelly is a special type of honey that is fed only to the queen bee, and to very young larvae of drone and worker bees.

3F Mosquitoes are, carrying malaria, sleeping sickness, etc. Insects aside, the animal that most frequently attacks people is the domestic dog – over 20 million attacks estimated worldwide per year, many times more than all wild animal attacks put together.

4T Galapagos penguins, in the Eastern Pacific Ocean.

5F The sperm whale and killer whale are much bigger.

6F Incredibly, there has never been a single scientifically confirmed human fatality from a piranha attack! Piranhas may devour a dead human body (e.g. drowned) but only kill smaller, more familiar prey.

7T Incredibly! The gastric-brooding frog of Australia does this. While the tadpoles are in the stomach, it is able to neutralise its stomach acid. The young are regurgitated as baby frogs. Now very rare.

8F Spitting cobras can blind temporarily, but never kill in this way.

9F Hippos kill the most. Even elephants and water buffalo kill more!

10T Praying mantis (*see image*), and some spiders do this.

6 Homework idea

During the presentations it is likely that the experts were not able to answer all the questions. Throw back the unanswered questions at them and tell them to try to find the answers for homework, either using the internet, a local library or a bookshop. Some students may even be inspired to research their chosen animal further and do a presentation.

Natural Born Killers

Fact File A: Sharks

What sharks eat

Sharks are sophisticated, careful killers. They have at least seven different senses (two more than us), 3000 teeth, and can smell blood from more than a mile away. Thanks to these incredible features, sharks very rarely attack unfamiliar prey. Although most sharks feed on fish, not all are predators. Some, including the three largest species, feed on tiny plankton. The great white shark often feeds on sea lions and other sea mammals.

Shark attacks on people

There were about 76 shark attacks on people in 2001, only five of which were fatal. In the same year, there were 4.5 million dog attacks on people in the USA alone, 18 of which resulted in death.

Which sharks attack humans and why

Only three species of sharks attack humans regularly. The majority of human attacks are due to great white sharks mistaking surfers for sea lions on the surface of the water, and only occasionally result in death. Occasionally, tiger sharks or bull (also called Zambezi) sharks may swim close to beaches and attack swimmers, especially if there is lots of noise and excitement.

Different types of shark and where they live

There are over 390 species of shark inhabiting seas worldwide, from the ice-covered Arctic and Antarctic Oceans to the warmest coral seas of the tropics, and even rivers. They have been around for over 450 million years, since before dinosaurs, making them one of the most successful animals on the planet in evolutionary terms. They range in size from the tiny pygmy shark, 10cm long, to the majestic, 15m-long whale shark and are some of the fastest swimmers of the sea – blue sharks and mako sharks can swim at up to 40km/h for short distances.

People attacks on sharks

Sharks have far more reason to fear people than we have to fear them. Over 150 million are killed every year, mostly for shark fin soup, a delicacy in China. 100 million are caught in fishing nets by mistake, and at least 20 species are endangered. Yet sharks are an extremely important part of the food chain, helping to keep fish numbers regulated and cleaning the sea of dead and dying animals. Just two reasons why we need to respect and conserve – not fear and hate – these beautiful predators.

Advice for avoiding shark attacks:

- *Never swim on your own – there's safety in numbers.*
- *Avoid places where the water suddenly gets deeper – this is where sharks often feed.*
- *Never swim with open cuts – sharks are very sensitive to blood.*
- *Don't wear shiny jewellery in the water – sharks may mistake jewellery for fish scales and attack.*
- *Don't swim at dawn or dusk – these are the natural feeding times of sharks.*
- *Be extremely careful when diving with the natural prey of large sharks, such as fish shoals or sea lions – always dive in teams, and follow the advice of local divers.*

Vocabulary check

sophisticated – very well-developed
prey – animals that are eaten by others
predator – any animal that kills other animals for food
species – type of animal
plankton – tiny animals and plants that live in the sea
sea lions – a sea mammal (*see picture*)
fatal – resulting in death
evolutionary – from evolution: the development of different types of animals over millions of years
delicacy – a highly-valued food
endangered – in danger of extinction
food chain – the link between predators and prey in the natural world
regulated – kept under control
conserve – protect and keep in good condition
scales – small plates on the skin of fish or reptiles
shoal – group (of fish)

Natural Born Killers

Fact File B: Snakes

Different types of snake

Snakes are one of the most diverse and widespread animal groups in the world, and they are also one of the most misunderstood. There are over 2500 different species of snake, but less than 500 of them are poisonous, and no more than 40 are responsible for human fatalities on a regular basis. The smallest species measure only a few centimetres long, the largest – the anaconda of South America may be up to nine metres in length.

Where snakes live and what they eat

The many amazing species, each with its own specialist prey and lifestyle, have made homes in a large variety of habitats, from the driest deserts to the open oceans. Most snakes live in places with low human populations. Snakes are cold-blooded reptiles, and so the only places they cannot survive are in arctic and mountain areas. 90% of snakes prey on amphibians such as frogs, small mammals such as mice or rats, and insects. Sea snakes eat fish and a few larger species such as the reticulated python of Asia or the anaconda are large enough to kill and eat deer or even crocodiles!

Snake attacks on people

Contrary to belief, snakes are scared of people and always try to avoid contact with us. Where poisonous snakes do come into regular contact with people (mainly in Africa, the Middle East and Asia), they are serious killers, although ironically this is usually due to people walking around barefoot and stepping on hiding or resting snakes. In these places there is rarely a hospital nearby or any transport, and the victims often die because ineffective traditional medicine is preferred to professional medical help. Despite this, of the 13 million snake bites estimated yearly, only about 30,000 result in death. The biggest killers are probably Russell's viper of Asia, the saw-scaled viper of the Middle East and the Indian cobra, each killing from 5,000–15,000 people each year.

Snake poison

The most poisonous snake in the world is probably the inland taipan of Australia, a single bite from it contains enough venom to kill almost 250,000 mice! Yet, despite the large number of highly venomous snakes living in Australia, fewer than five people are killed per year there from snake bites thanks to good footwear and a low population. There are other very dangerous poisonous snakes such as the king cobra of India, which can kill an elephant with one bite, or the spitting cobra, which can fire its venom into the eyes, causing temporary blindness.

People attacks on snakes

Because snakes have such a bad reputation, they are often killed on sight by people, and over 100 species are now endangered. This is a great shame, as they represent one of the most beautiful and varied families in the animal kingdom. What's more, the complex chemical makeup of their venom is of great use to science and is used in medicine for treating strokes, blood clotting, epilepsy, Alzheimer's disease and even breast cancer.

Snake myths

Snakes cannot milk cows or roll like wheels down hills. Snakes do not dance – they are deaf. The black mamba is the fastest snake, but can only move at the same speed as a running man (15 mph), not as fast as a running horse! There are no evil snakes that ever attack people on purpose.

Advice for treating snake bites:

- *Don't panic. A faster heartbeat will cause the poison to spread faster. Remember – only 50% of snake bites contain venom, and less than 1% are fatal.*
- *Keep the infected leg or arm below the heart.*
- *Isolate the wound and stop the blood flow to the rest of the body using a piece of material tied tightly around the leg or arm.*
- *If possible, don't allow the victim to walk. Always bring the transport to the victim.*
- *Do not attempt to cut or suck out the venom. It is usually ineffective and likely to speed up blood circulation.*

Vocabulary check

diverse – with many different types
widespread – found all over the world
species – type of animal
fatalities – deaths
prey (n) – animals that snakes eat
habitat – the type of place where a species lives
prey on – kill and eat
amphibians – a group of animals that live in or near water, including frogs
barefoot – without shoes
estimated – guessed
venom – snake poison
endangered – in danger of extinction

Natural Born Killers

Fact File C: Bears

Different types of bear

There are eight different species of bear, living across much of the world. They range from the small, honey-loving sun bear, weighing up to 65kg and the famous giant panda to the fearsome 'grizzly' brown bear and the massive polar bear, which, at 800kg, is the largest of all land carnivores.

What bears eat

Although polar bears feed almost entirely on seals, most other species of bear eat a wide variety of food, including berries, fruit, grasses, honey, eggs, fish and deer. The panda is an exception, which, despite having the teeth of a carnivore, eats only bamboo and other plants. As large predators, bears are important members of the food chain, able to feed on almost any food that becomes over-abundant.

Human attacks on bears

For thousands of years, bears have lived alongside us, and have been persecuted and hunted by us for their skins or internal organs (used in traditional medicine). All eight species of bear are endangered across much, if not all of their range. We all know of the rarity and the vulnerability of the panda, with only 1,000 of these beautiful animals left, but not many of us are aware of the fight for survival of the spectacled bear in the Andes of South America or the strange sloth bear of India. Both species may be down to less than 10,000 individuals.

Bear attacks on people

Of course bears have always constituted a threat towards people, but due to misunderstanding and superstition, that threat has been greatly exaggerated. In North America there were only two deaths from bear attacks in 2001, and only 18 in the whole of the 1990s. Worldwide, figures can be estimated at between four and eight human deaths per year, many of which occur as a result of people trying to chase bears away from crops or disturbing mothers with cubs. Every year millions of meetings between wild bears and people occur and all but a few pass without harm to the human. Many result in the needless death of the bear.

What bears can do

Bears can climb trees easily and quickly. They are excellent swimmers, especially polar bears. They can also walk on their back legs and fish for salmon in rivers. Bears love honey, and risk real danger to get it. Bears can't actually see very well, and only have black and white vision. Their sense of smell is excellent, so be careful if you are walking with food in bear country!

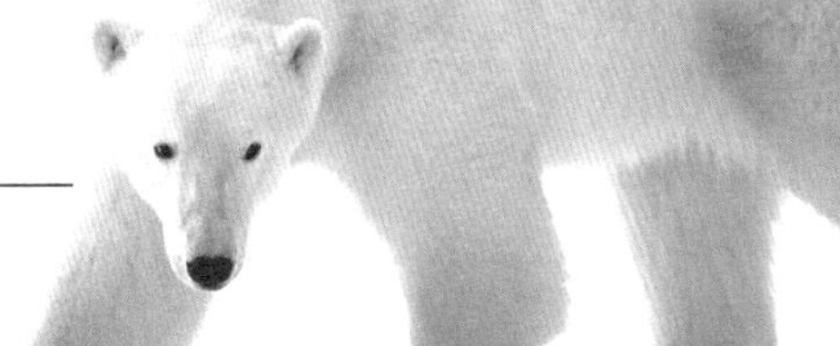

If you see a bear, follow this advice:

- *Try not to surprise bears. They will avoid you if they hear or smell you coming.*
- *Do not block a bear's exit route and never stand between a mother and a cub.*
- *If you surprise a brown bear, stay calm, drop something in front of you like your hat or gloves and back away slowly.*
- *If a bear approaches you slowly, or charges at you, stand up tall, make a noise, and wave your hands to make yourself as big as possible. Shaking a plastic bag can be very effective in scaring bears off!*
- *Never run from a bear because this may provoke a charge.*
- *Playing dead may work with brown bears, but not with black bears. Don't do it unless you are sure you can tell the difference!*
- *Do not leave food about in bear country and never feed bears, even if they seem tame.*

Vocabulary check

species – type of animal
carnivores – animals that eat meat
seals – a type of sea mammal (*see picture*)
over-abundant – too plentiful
persecuted – hunted and killed without reason
endangered – in danger of extinction
range – total area in which a species lives
vulnerability – weakness (as a species)
constituted a threat – been dangerous
superstition – a traditional folk belief (probably untrue)
estimated – guessed
crops – rice, wheat, corn, etc.
cubs – baby bears
charge (v) – run at (in attack)
provoke – cause something / someone to react
tame – not wild, domestic

Natural Born Killers

Fact File D: Tigers

Different types of tiger

There are five different species of tiger: the Bengal (or Indian) Tiger, the Siberian (or Amur) Tiger, the Indochinese Tiger, the South China Tiger, the Sumatran Tiger. Three other species have become extinct since the 1930s. The largest of all tigers is the Siberian Tiger, and it can be up to 300kg in weight. The smallest and also the rarest is the South China Tiger, only 20–30 of which survive in the wild. All tigers have stripes to provide camouflage in long grass and forests.

Where tigers live and what they eat

All five species of tiger live in Asia, and have adapted to life in both cold environments (the Siberian Tiger can survive winter temperatures of -30°C) and tropical rainforests. Just over 100 years ago, the Caspian Tiger was also widespread over the deserts of the Middle East and Central Asia. Tigers like water and are good swimmers. All tiger species naturally prey on large land animals, such as deer, wild cows and pigs. They almost always attack from behind, stalking their prey carefully before pouncing and killing it. Tigers can eat a lot of meat at once, up to 18kg, and don't usually eat unfamiliar prey, such as people or domestic animals.

Tiger attacks on people

Despite being often called 'man-eaters', there are probably only 40–70 people killed each year by tigers worldwide. It is said that once a tiger has tasted human blood, it will probably try to kill again. But the simple fact is that nearly all 'man-eating' tigers are old and sick and too slow to catch their natural prey. The Sunderbans mangrove forest in India is the place where the largest number of tiger attacks occur. In recent years, a simple idea has reduced tiger attacks on people greatly. Because tigers always attack from behind, the local people were advised to wear masks on the back of their heads, so that the tiger thinks it is facing its prey and will not attack. This has halved tiger attacks in recent years.

Threats to tigers from humans

At the start of this century there were probably 100,000 wild tigers. Today there are less than 7,000. This is due to two main threats: poaching and habitat loss. Poaching of tigers is very common. In India over 100 are killed every year and their body parts (eyes, brains, whiskers, tails and bones) are sold for use in traditional Chinese medicine. The medicinal effect of these body parts is minimal, but they definitely don't do the tigers any good. Habitat loss is occurring all across Asia because the forests where the tigers live are being chopped down for wood or for farmland. Each tiger needs between 30 and 300 square kilometres of forest to survive and raise young. What's more, these forests need to be linked together so that the tigers can breed successfully. In India, with its fast-growing population, such forests are becoming fewer and smaller every year.

White tigers

White tigers are found naturally, but they are extremely rare. They are not Siberian tigers, they are pale Bengal tigers with light brown stripes and blue eyes. The white colour is caused by a rare gene. Often white tigers find it difficult to survive in the wild because they cannot catch prey so easily, and so most white tigers live in zoos.

Advice for avoiding tiger attacks:

The only people at serious risk of tiger attack are villagers in India and other parts of Asia, who must travel through tiger country to find food or firewood. In general, the following advice has helped the people of the Sunderbans to reduce the risk of tiger attacks:

- *Never travel into the forest on your own – tigers prefer to attack single prey, never groups.*
- *Make plenty of noise – tigers are most dangerous when they are surprised.*
- *Do not bend down or sit for a long time in one place – if you do, wear a mask on the back of your head.*
- *If you find a tiger meal, leave the area immediately and warn others. The tiger will probably come back to finish it soon. It may already be watching you!*
- *If you see a tiger at a distance, never run away. The tiger will think you are prey. Make lots of noise and stay where you are. Throwing rocks and waving sticks might also frighten the tiger off.*

Vocabulary check

species – type of animal
become extinct – all the animals in the species die
stripes – dark lines on the side of a tiger
camouflage – skin patterns that help an animal hide
widespread – found over a very large area
prey (n) – animals that the tiger hunts; *prey on* (v) kill and eat
stalking – following secretly
pouncing – jumping out in a surprise attack
mask – a false face you wear to hide your identity
threat – danger (often in the future)
poach – hunt animals illegally
habitat – the place where an animal lives
whiskers – long hairs on a cat's face
breed (v) – make baby tigers

Natural Born Killers

Amazing Animals Quiz

Work in groups. Decide if the following statements are true or false:

1. A type of bird called the swift sleeps in the air.
2. Royal jelly, produced by honeybees, is worth more per kilo than gold.
3. Snakes are the biggest human killers of the animal world.
4. Penguins can be found on the equator.
5. The world's largest predator is the great white shark.
6. Piranhas kill an average of 20 people per year in the rivers of South America.
7. Some frogs swallow their eggs which then develop in their stomachs.
8. Some snakes can kill people by spitting their venom.
9. In Africa the most dangerous large mammals to people are lions.
10. Some animals eat their partner after sex.

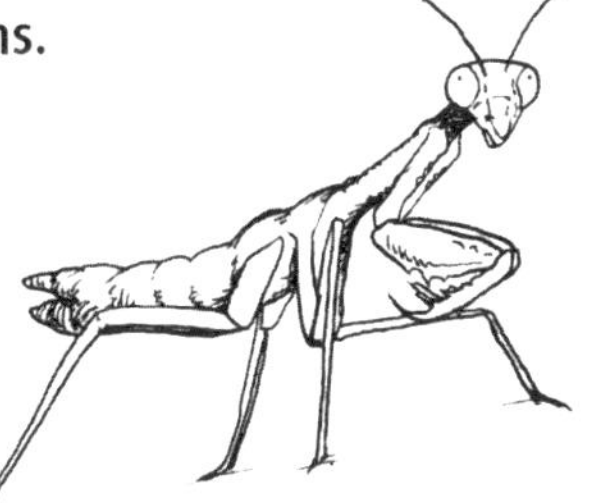

Natural Born Killers

Amazing Animals Quiz

Work in groups. Decide if the following statements are true or false:

1. A type of bird called the swift sleeps in the air.
2. Royal jelly, produced by honeybees, is worth more per kilo than gold.
3. Snakes are the biggest human killers of the animal world.
4. Penguins can be found on the equator.
5. The world's largest predator is the great white shark.
6. Piranhas kill an average of 20 people per year in the rivers of South America.
7. Some frogs swallow their eggs which then develop in their stomachs.
8. Some snakes can kill people by spitting their venom.
9. In Africa the most dangerous large mammals to people are lions.
10. Some animals eat their partner after sex.

18 "It's the Way I Tell 'em": Teacher's notes

Topic focus	Jokes / humour; Culture & cultural stereotypes; Stories
Grammar / Functional focus	Present simple in jokes (historic present); Direct speech; Spoken discourse markers in jokes
Level / Number of students	Intermediate – Advanced / Minimum six students
Time	50–60 minutes (Extension 5–15 minutes)

Preparation

Copy the main worksheet (1 per student), the skeletons and original jokes (2 copies per 12 students). Cut up as indicated.

1 Teacher tells joke

Hand out the main worksheet and tell the students that you are going to tell them a joke. Read through Stage 1 on the worksheet. Then tell the students one of the jokes in this unit (or one of your own). Tell it well, using mime, detail, etc. The students then discuss questions A–D in pairs. Get feedback. We usually use present simple to tell jokes, rather than past tenses. Make sure the students notice this.

2 The key factors

Pre-teach *punchline* (the final, funny line of the joke). Read through Stage 2 on the worksheet with them and tell them to work in pairs (5 mins). Get different groups to compare their results with each other.

3 Joke skeleton – optional

Look at the beginning of the joke skeleton with the students and elicit the first sentence (below). Tell them to listen carefully to the joke, and then to complete the skeleton.

> **The Quickest Way Joke**
> A newspaper seller is standing on the corner of Oxford Street (in London), and a tourist comes up to him and asks: "What's the quickest way to get to Trafalgar Square from here?" The newspaper seller looks at the tourist and says: "How are you travelling – on foot or by car?" "By car," says the tourist. "Good," says the newspaper seller, "That's definitely the quickest way."

Students should discuss the questions in Stage 3. They could also re-tell the joke if time permits. With lower level students, leave out this stage, and move straight on to Stage 4, giving them the original jokes to work from.

4 Students prepare to tell jokes

Read through Stage 4 with the students and hand out the joke skeletons, two copies of the same skeleton per pair. If you have over 12 students, create some groups of three students instead of pairs. Give them ten minutes to prepare, reminding them to include all the factors they thought were important in Stage 2 in their joke (e.g. using body language in the joke, etc.).

Note: *If the students don't understand the skeleton, give them the original joke.*

5 Students tell jokes

Get the whole class to stand up, mingle and tell their joke to at least four other students. Because two (or more) students have learnt the same joke, they may meet someone who has already heard their joke. Teach them: "I've heard that one before."

Optional: *Draw a 'laughometer' on the board and record which students get the biggest laughs.*

6 Discussion

In groups of three to four, students discuss the questions. Get feedback at the end, eliciting some of their favourite jokes.

Extension: Joke race

Split the class into two teams and put them in two lines facing the board. Give the two students next to the board a pen (or chalk). Tell them that you are going to give a short joke to the last student in each line, and that they must whisper it to the student in front of them, who must pass it on until it gets to the student by the board, who writes it on the board. The first team to write their joke correctly wins. Remind them that they can only whisper. Show two different jokes (*paired below*) to the last two students at the same time, and start them off! Do all three pairs if you have time.

What happens when you jog backwards? You put on weight.	How do you keep an idiot waiting? I'll tell you tomorrow.
Hard work pays off in the future. Laziness pays off NOW!	I like kids but I don't think I could eat a whole one.
Always remember you're unique – just like everyone else.	If practice makes perfect, and nobody's perfect, why practise?

"It's the Way I Tell 'em"

Stage 1

Your teacher is going to tell you a joke. Listen to it to see if you understand it and if you think it's funny. After you've heard the joke, answer the following questions:

A) Do you think it's funny? Why? Why not?

B) If yes, what makes the joke funny?

C) If no, could you change the joke to make it funny?

D) What was the main verb tense the teacher used to tell the joke?

Stage 2

Which of these factors do you think are important in a good joke? Cross out any that are not important and put the others in order, starting with 1 for the most important factor.

- ☐ using body language when telling the joke
- ☐ remembering every word of the joke
- ☐ an unexpected punchline (ending)
- ☐ looking directly in the eyes of your audience
- ☐ enjoying telling the joke yourself
- ☐ keeping a straight face while you tell the joke
- ☐ saying the punchline quickly
- ☐ giving plenty of detail
- ☐ clear pronunciation and regular rhythm
- ☐ laughing at the mistakes or stupidity of others
- ☐ ?

Compare with other students when you have finished.

Stage 3

Now listen to another joke. Continue the following 'joke skeleton':

Newspaper seller / corner / Oxford St / tourist / comes up – ...

Why is a joke skeleton useful? Have you (or your friends) ever forgotten the order of the facts in a joke?

Stage 4

Now it's your turn to tell a joke. Work together with another student. The teacher will give you a joke skeleton. You have ten minutes to do the following:

✔ Read through it and check that you understand the joke.

✔ Think of all the extra details that will make the joke really funny! (Don't write them down – try to remember them.)

✔ Is there any vocabulary that other students may not understand? Can you explain it before you tell the joke? How?

✔ In pairs, practise retelling the joke. Don't forget to pay attention to the factors you looked at in Stage 2 above.

Stage 5

Now, both of you stand up and tell the joke to other students in your class. Try to tell it from memory, using only your joke skeleton for help. Remember which other students find it funny and which don't.

Discussion

- Which of the jokes did you find funny? Which weren't funny?
- Who do you think told their joke well? Why?
- Did you find any of the jokes offensive?
- Do you think that people from different countries find different jokes funny? Why?
- Think of one or two jokes from your country and try translating them into English. Tell them to the other students. Do you think that these jokes would be funny to an English speaker?

"It's the Way I Tell 'em": Joke Skeletons

Two Hunters Joke (An international survey in 2002 named this the funniest joke in the world)

Don't forget to check: hunter, operator, gunshot

2 hunters /middle / big forest / one / has a heart attack. Maybe dead? Other hunter / mobile phone / calls / ambulance. "Friend / heart attack! / dead? What / do?" / operator: "Calm down, etc. First / make sure / definitely dead" / hunter puts phone down / seconds later / 'BANG!' – gun firing. Hunter / picks up phone: "OK, now what?"

Antiques Collector Joke

Don't forget to check: antiques collector, bowl (n)

Antiques collector / one day / old shop / dirty old cat drinking milk / bowl very old / antique / worth £ millions. V. excited! Idea / asks owner / buy cat / explains why. £10 – no / £20 – no / £50 – no / £100 – yes. £20 more / buy bowl? No / bowl not for sale / lucky bowl / this week / sold 68 cats!

Three Builders Joke

Don't forget to check: lunchbox, funeral

three builders at work / lunch break / top floor / building site / Bob opens lunchbox: cheese sandwiches / "I'm sick of cheese/ if / cheese sandwiches tomorrow / jump / kill myself" Bill opens lunchbox: ham sandwiches / "hate ham / if / ham again / kill myself too" Tom: egg sandwiches – "if / egg again / kill myself too" next day / all nervous / open lunchboxes / Bob / cheese / jumps / dead / Bill / ham / jumps / dead / Tom / egg / jumps too / three days later / funeral of 3 men / 3 wives / crying / Bill's wife: "why didn't he tell me / didn't like cheese?" / Bill's wife agrees: "I wish / told me" / Tom's wife / confused: "I don't understand / my husband always made his own sandwiches"

Desert Island Joke

Don't forget to check: lamp, polish (v), genie, wish,

3 men / all on desert island / 11 years / no ships / pass / lose hope / rescue / one day / on beach / find lamp / 1 picks up / polishes / genie appears / "Your wish is my command" / 3 wishes / 1 each / 1st man smiles / "I wish / in my country / garden / summer / with wife / nice drink / barbecue, etc." / wish comes true / disappears / 2nd man thinks / "I wish / in my country / nice restaurant / with girlfriend, etc." / wish comes true / disappears / 3rd man / looks around / sad / confused / says "never see / friends / again / wish they hadn't left without saying goodbye"

Three Unemployed Soldiers Joke

Don't forget to check: spy / sergeant, brave, follow orders, shoot, bullets

3 unemployed soldiers / apply / job / spies / at interview / sergeant: "must be brave / be spy / if / want to be a spy / must follow any orders / we have special test / must do / what I tell you" / gives guns to 3 soldiers / "go home / shoot / 1st person you see / return tomorrow / if / you follow orders / give job / 3 soldiers / worried / but leave with guns / next day / come back / 1st soldier: "sorry / couldn't do it / went home / wife smiling / dinner on table / failed" gives gun back / leaves / 2nd soldier: "failed also / son opened door / asked / help / with homework / couldn't shoot" gives gun back / goes home / 3rd soldier: "got home / went upstairs / mother-in-law / in bed asleep / shot / but no bullets in gun / so / picked her up / threw out / window"

Three Trees Joke

Don't forget to check: parrot, monkey, stone

war Africa / 3 soldiers alone / enemy soldiers see them / chase / 5 miles / 3 soldiers decide / hide in 3 big trees / enemy soldiers arrive / can't find / see 3 big trees / hear noises / something moving /decide / throw stones into trees / 1st tree/ throw stone / 1st soldier makes noise: "caw caw" (like parrot) / enemies think: parrot / 2nd tree / same / throw stone / 2nd soldier / noise "ooh, ooh" (like monkey) / enemies think: monkey / 3rd tree / 3rd soldier / throw stone / "moo" (like cow)!

"It's the Way I Tell 'em": Original Jokes

Two Hunters Joke (An international survey in 2002 named this the funniest joke in the world)

Two hunters are out in a big forest when one of them has a heart attack. He doesn't seem to be breathing and his eyes are open. The other hunter takes out his mobile phone and calls for an ambulance. "My friend has had a heart attack! I think he's dead. What shall I do?", he says. The operator says: "Calm down, don't panic! First, let's make sure he's dead." The operator is about to explain how to check for signs of life when she notices that the hunter has put the phone down. A few seconds later she hears the 'BANG!' of a gun firing. The hunter comes back to the phone, and says: "OK, now what?"

Antiques Collector Joke

An antiques collector is walking through the city when he notices a dirty old cat lapping milk from a bowl in the doorway of an old shop. He suddenly notices that the saucer is a 3,000 year old Chinese Ming Dynasty bowl and worth over £1,000,000. He gets very excited and thinks carefully about what to do. He has an idea and walks calmly into the store. He greets the owner and explains that he has too many mice in his house and needs a cat now to catch them. He offers the owner £10 for the cat. The store owner replies, "I'm sorry, but the cat isn't for sale." The collector says, "Please, I need a cat quickly. I'll give you £20 for the cat." Again the owner refuses. The collector offers him £50 then £100. Finally the owner says "Sold," He takes the £100 and gives the cat to the collector. The collector continues, "Hey, if I give you another £20, could you let me have that old bowl? The cat's used to it and you don't need it anymore." And the owner says, "Sorry my friend, but that's my lucky bowl. So far this week I've sold sixty-eight cats!"

Three Builders Joke

There were three builders at work, all on their lunch break, eating sandwiches on the top floor of a building site. "Oh no," says Bob, "Cheese sandwiches! I'm sick of cheese. If my wife puts cheese in my sandwiches tomorrow, I'm going to jump out of the window and kill myself." Bill opens his lunchbox: "Oh no! Ham sandwiches. If I get ham again, I'm going to kill myself too." Tom opens his lunchbox: "Egg sandwiches! That's it. If I get egg again, I'll kill myself too." The next day, they're all nervous, and one by one they open their lunchboxes – Bob gets cheese, and jumps, Bill gets ham, and jumps and Tom gets egg and he jumps too. Three days later it's their funeral. Bob's wife, crying, says: "Why didn't he tell me that he didn't like cheese?" Bill's wife agrees, "I know. If only he had told me!" Tom's wife looks at them confused: "I don't understand it. My husband always made his own sandwiches."

Desert Island Joke

Three men have all been on a desert island for eleven years. No ships have passed and they have lost all hope of ever being rescued. Then one day they are walking along the beach and they find a lamp in the sand. One of them picks it up, starts to polish it and suddenly a genie appears. "Your wish is my command," says the genie. "I will give you three wishes, that's one wish for each of you." The first man smiles and says "Oh I wish I was back home in my country, sitting in my garden on a summer afternoon with a nice drink in my hand." The genie nods, and the first man disappears in a cloud of smoke. The second man laughs and says: "Oh I wish I was back in my country sitting in a nice restaurant with my girlfriend." The genie nods, and the second man also disappears in a cloud of smoke. The genie turns to the third man, who looks around, and seems a little bit confused. He says: "What a shame! I shall never see my two good friends again. I wish they hadn't left without saying goodbye."

Three Unemployed Soldiers Joke

Three unemployed soldiers decide to apply to become spies. They arrive for the interview and the sergeant looks at them. "I don't think any of you are brave enough to be a spy, but if you want you can take the test." The soldiers thank him and he continues: "To be a spy you have to be ready to follow any order I give you." He gives a gun to each of them and says: "Now go home and shoot the first person you see. Come back tomorrow. If you've followed my orders I'll give you all the job." The three unemployed soldiers look worried, and leave without saying anything. The next day they come back. The first one says: "I'm sorry. I couldn't do it. I got home, and there was my lovely wife ready to greet me, with my dinner on the table. I failed the test." The second one says: "I failed as well. My 8-year-old son opened the door and asked me to help him with his homework. I couldn't shoot him!" The third one says: "When I got home, I went upstairs and found my mother-in-law asleep in bed. I fired the gun, but there were no bullets in it! So I picked her up and threw her out the window."

Three Trees Joke

During the war, three soldiers are all in the African jungle being followed by enemy soldiers. The enemies are getting closer and closer so the three soldiers decide to hide in three big trees. The enemies arrive at the trees, and stop, hearing noises and seeing movement in the trees. They throw a stone into the first tree, where the first soldier is hiding. "Caw, caw," (like a parrot) is heard from the tree. "It's just a parrot," the enemies decide, and they move to the next tree, where the second soldier is hiding, and throw a stone into it. They hear the sound "ooh, ooh, ooh," (just like a monkey). "It's just a monkey," they decide and move on to the third tree, where the third soldier is hiding. They throw a stone and hear: "Mooooo"....

19 What Happened Next?: Teacher's notes

Topic focus	Storytelling; Crime and law; Mistakes; Cars
Grammar / Functional focus	Narrative tenses; *will / might* for prediction; Agreeing and disagreeing; Expressing opinions
Level / Number of students	Intermediate to Advanced / Minimum four students
Time	30–40 minutes (Extension 15 minutes)

Preparation

Copy and cut up the story extracts A–F, the conclusion, the vocabulary check and the group discussion sheets (1 copy of each per group of 3–4 students).

1 Suggested lead-in

Write the following words on the board:

supermarket mistake coat
back seat car park football

Tell the students that all of these words are from the first part of a story. Put them into groups of three to four and tell them to try to predict what happens in the story.

2 Vocabulary check (Intermediate only)

Hand out the vocabulary check reference sheets before you begin, one per group. Explain that any difficult words in the story are underlined and explained on this sheet.

3 Reading the story extracts

Hand out extract A to each group. Students read the extract. When they come to the four options at the end, give them three minutes to discuss and try to agree on what happens next in the story. Monitor to make sure that they discuss all four options carefully before making their decisions. Give each group a team name or number and record their choices on the board. Next hand out extract B and let them look quickly to see which option was correct. Score one point to any groups who predicted correctly. Repeat with extract C. Continue in this way through to extract F, keeping note of the scores as you go along (*see boardwork example opposite*).

Suggestion: *The students could take it in turns to read the story extracts aloud.*

Answers A3 B1 C2 D4 E2

4 Extract F and the conclusion

After the students have read extract F, give them five minutes to predict how the story will end. One member of each group recounts their version to the class. Give three bonus points for the most accurate prediction. Hand out the conclusion for them to read. At the end they have to choose the original name for the story (one point).

Answer 4 Two wrongs do not make a right!

Extension: Group discussion

Hand out the group discussion sheets and let them discuss the questions in their groups.

Tip: *Try re-grouping the students for this activity.*

Students could write an account of one of their own big mistakes for homework.

The idea for 'What happened next' can be used with a variety of short stories to make reading a more enjoyable, interactive activity. Try creating multiple choice questions for other texts you are reading with the students.

Boardwork Example

	Team 1	*Team 2*	*Team 3*
A	*2* ✘	*3* ✔	*1* ✘
B	*1* ✔	*4* ✘	*1* ✔
C	*2* ✔	*2* ✔	*2* ✔
D	*4* ✔	*3* ✘	*1* ✘
E	*3* ✘	*2* ✔	*2* ✔
F		*3 points*	
Conclusion	*4* ✔	*1* ✘	*2* ✘

What Happened Next? Extract A

It was a Saturday morning at eleven o'clock when Colin picked me up from my flat. As usual, we drove down to the big supermarket just out of town in his silver Peugeot 206 to do our shopping. As usual we chatted about football all the time – we both support the same team. When we had finished, we walked back to the car, still talking about football. We put our bags of shopping into the boot of the car, got in and set off, still chatting. We got back to my flat, and it was only when we started unloading the shopping that we noticed something strange. Colin said:

"Don't forget your coat, Jason. It's on the back seat."

"I didn't bring a coat," I said.

"Well it's not mine! Actually, neither is that book on the back seat."

What happened next?

1 Somebody had broken into the car and put the things onto the back seat.
2 Colin's girlfriend had been having an affair. The things belonged to her lover.
3 We had taken the wrong car from the car park.
4 There was somebody hiding under the coat.

What Happened Next? Extract B

At that moment, we suddenly realised that the car wasn't Colin's! It was a silver Peugeot 206, just like Colin's, but it was a completely different car. The number plate was different, as were the things on the back seat.

"Oh my God!" said Colin, "We've got the wrong car."

"That's impossible. How did your keys open the door?"

"That sometimes can happen, if it's the same model. But we'll have to take it back."

"You're right," I said, "but now that we're here, let's put my shopping in the flat."

So Colin gave me a hand to carry the shopping up to my flat, which was on the eighth floor of a block of flats.

What happened next?

1 When we got back to the car, it had been stolen.
2 We decided to call the police from my flat.
3 When we got back to the car, the police were waiting for us.
4 The shopping was not ours.

What Happened Next? Extract C

The lift in my block of flats hasn't worked for about three years, so Colin and I walked up and then down the stairs from the eighth floor. When we got to the car park five minutes later, we noticed the space where we'd parked the car was empty.

"I don't believe it. It's been stolen!" Colin cried out.

"Didn't you lock it?" I asked.

"No! We were only gone a couple of minutes!"

"Oh no!" I said, "What are we going to do now?"

We both sat down on the pavement in complete despair, and started to discuss our options.

What happened next?

1 We decided to go straight to the police.
2 We decided to go back and get my car without telling the police.
3 We decided to find the thief ourselves.
4 Colin had left his mobile phone in the car. We decided to call it.

What Happened Next? Extract D

"If we go to the police, it will be very difficult to explain the situation." I said. "How can we prove that we didn't steal the car?"

"But I've got a car," said Colin, "Why would we steal it?"

"I don't know... To sell it," I suggested.

"OK. But if we don't go back, the police will be looking for us."

"No, they won't. They'll be looking for the car." I explained, "And the car really has been stolen. End of problem! Why bother telling them that we're involved?"

We spent another few minutes in silence before Colin said:

"I suppose we could go back in a few hours and get my car. When the car park's empty, and everyone's gone home."

"I know it sounds terrible, but I think it's the best option. You could go back this evening after it gets dark," I explained.

"Aren't you coming with me?"

"No! It wasn't my mistake."

"How can you say that? We both made the mistake!" Colin was clearly worried.

"OK. I'll come with you," I agreed, reluctantly.

What happened next?

1 We saw the stolen car on the news – It had been involved in a robbery.
2 We went back to the car park but Colin's car wasn't there.
3 We went back to the car park, but Colin had lost his keys. We had to break into his car.
4 We went back to the car park and Colin's car was still there.

What Happened Next? Extract E

At about eight o'clock that evening we left my flat, dressed in dark clothes. We were both extremely nervous. We caught the number 93 bus to the supermarket. I put a black hat on and pulled it down low to cover most of my face. Colin pulled his hood up. When we got to the car park, we looked over the wall. There were only three cars there – an old Ford Fiesta, a dirty white van and the silver Peugeot 206 that we had come for. We had a good look to check for security guards, and as soon as we were sure it was safe, Colin said:

"Let's go for it!"

We jumped over the wall and walked quickly to the car. Colin put his key into the lock, opened the doors and we got in and drove off.

"We've done it!" he said.

What happened next?

1 We realised that we weren't in Colin's car, but in the stolen car.

2 The police were hiding, waiting for us. We were arrested.

3 The owner of the car we took from the supermarket was waiting, hiding in the back seat.

4 We found a note in the car.

What Happened Next? Extract F

"Don't speak too soon," I said, "We're not out of the car park yet."

Just at that moment, a blue flashing light switched on in front of us. It was a police car, and it was blocking the exit from the car park.

"Oh no!" I said.

Colin just froze. We stopped the car and waited. Two policemen got out, and so did the security guard from the supermarket. They walked over. The security guard looked at us and nodded:

"They're the ones."

"Could you both step out of the car, please," said one of the policemen.

As soon as we got out, they handcuffed us and told us we were under arrest.

"But what for?" said Colin.

"For stealing a silver Peugeot 206," said the other officer. "We've got you on video, so I recommend you keep quiet. Anything you say may be used as evidence."

How did the story finish?

What Happened Next? The Conclusion

When we got to the police station they separated us straight away. After about one hour in a police cell, I was interviewed by a woman detective who was very nice, and seemed prepared to listen to what I had to say. I explained the first mistake at the supermarket, and then told her how the car had been stolen outside my flat. She nodded and looked at me for about ten seconds.

"Why should we believe you? How can you prove you didn't steal the other car? And how can you prove that the car was stolen outside your flat?"

"That's the problem," I said, "I can't prove anything. But that's why we came back for Colin's car."

"Two wrongs do not make a right. Didn't your parents ever teach you that?"

"Yes... But..."

"You are a very fortunate young man. Fortunate that you have told me the truth, and fortunate that the car that was stolen from your flat was recovered by the police about an hour ago. We also got the man who stole it."

"Oh, my God! Really?"

"Yes. But we couldn't understand why he claimed that he stole it from the flat, not from the supermarket. You two have just explained the riddle!"

"So that's it, then! We're free to go!"

"Not quite. The car was crashed after a police chase. The thief didn't have a licence, or any insurance. And what's more, you weren't insured to drive that car either. But someone is going to have to pay for the repair. The owner is prepared to drop any charges against you two if you pick up the repair bill."

"How much is it going to cost?" I asked, nervously.

"About £500 at least."

"Oh no!" I said and realised that it had probably been the most unlucky day of my life!!!

What was the original name of the story?

1 The most unlucky day of my life

2 Car crime

3 206 – my unlucky number

4 Two wrongs do not make a right

What Happened Next?

Vocabulary check

All of the underlined words from the story are explained below:

pick someone up – to collect someone in your car
unload – to take things out of or off something
give someone a hand – to help someone
despair (n) – complete sadness
Why bother (+ verb + ing) – there is no point (doing something)
reluctantly – without wanting to do it
flashing – like a light going on and off
blocking – standing or lying in the way
nod (v) – to move your head up and down (meaning 'Yes')
evidence – information to show a criminal is guilty
separate (adj) – different (not together)
cell – room in a prison / jail
fortunate – lucky
recover – to find or get
claim (v) – to say (that something is true)
riddle – a difficult problem (often in the form of a short poem or sentence)
police chase – when the police follow a suspect or criminal at high speed
insurance – money paid to a company to cover the cost of accidents etc.
drop (the) charges – not take you to court

(car) boot

block of flats

hood

handcuffs

What Happened Next?

Group discussion

- Did the story have the same conclusion as yours?
- Was your ending more interesting or more unexpected?
- Do you think it's a true story?
- What do you think the moral (the lesson to learn) of the story is?
- Have you ever made any big mistakes... as a child? / teenager? / adult?
- Have you ever got into trouble with... the police? / your parents?

  What did you do? Why did you do it?
  How did it end? What did you learn from it?

20 The Ghost of the Séance: Teacher's notes

Topic focus Crime and detective stories; Houses and furniture

Grammar / Functional focus Grammar revision (all areas); Narrative tenses, especially past continuous; *There was / were* for past tense description

Level / Number of students Intermediate to Advanced / Minimum six students

Time 60–80 minutes depending on level and time limits set

Comments

This activity is a good way to round off a course of study. The *Right or Wrong Grammar* tests 14 key grammar points. You can also write your own, based on what you've been studying. The story itself is entertaining and inspires discussion and debate. The activity can be used with any number of students from 6 to 106, and has been adapted for social programme parties! (see **Alternative ideas**)

Time note: *If you feel that the activity may take more than one lesson, you could give the students the background text to read for homework.*

Preparation

Copy the main story sheet, the task instructions and the clues (one copy of all for each team of 3–4 students). Cut up as indicated. You could get hold of some scary music and a few Sherlock Holmes pictures / props!

1 Suggested lead-in

Ask the students what they know about Sherlock Holmes: His job? (*Detective*) His address? (*221B Baker Street*) His assistant? (*Dr Watson*) His appearance? (*Tall, slim, pipe, funny hat,* etc.) His personality? (*very intelligent, logical, played the violin,* etc.) Tell them that they are going to try to solve one of the most difficult Sherlock Holmes mysteries, and at the same time revise their grammar.

2 The story so far

Divide the students into teams of 3–4 and hand out the *Ghost of the Séance* story sheet and the task instructions, one per team. Pre-teach: *séance* and *medium*. Students read the story (7–10 mins).

3 Clarifying the task

Read through the task instructions with them. Emphasise that they should choose carefully which clues to go for first, using the clue list. Set a time limit (30–45 minutes) and tell them that at the end they must provide their versions of the solution. Explain that you will come round the teams every five minutes and they will have the chance to win a clue. Write the following question on the board for discussion: *Who do you think had a motive to kill James?*

4 Winning clues

While they're still discussing the above question, go round from team to team with the *Right or Wrong Grammar* sentences. Each team should choose a clue. Read out the corresponding grammar sentence. They must decide if it is correct or wrong. Give them a few seconds to confer (if they think it is wrong, they should correct it). If they guess correctly, give them the corresponding clue. If they guess wrongly, they don't win any clue this time. Continue going round the teams in this way. They usually need a new clue every five minutes. When there are ten minutes left, stop going round and get them to concentrate on solving the crime.

Alternative idea: *You can hand out the sentences if you wish. This tends to work better with bigger classes (over 16 students) or if the room is small and students may overhear another team's response to the grammar sentences.*

5 The teams present their solutions

The teams each nominate a presenter who comes up to the front of the class. Ask each to explain: *Who was the murderer? Why did they do it? How did they do it?* Different teams may agree on the murderer, but rarely on the details. Once they finish, move on to the next stage, without yet telling them which team has won.

6 The solution

Hand out the solution sheets, and read it out aloud. It should be clear which team was closest to the correct solution. If none of the teams chose Rachael as the murderer, award first place for the most creative solution. If two or more teams chose Rachael, award the prize to the team who provided the most accurate explanation of how she did it.

Alternative ideas for using Ghost of the Séance

1 Instead of the *Right or Wrong Grammar* sentences, you could use 14 puzzles (observation, riddles, deduction, memory tests, crosswords etc.), putting them on the walls of the classroom.

2 For a big end-of-term activity, use puzzles. Merge classes of different levels together. Put the puzzles up on the walls of the classrooms all around the school and choose one room for 'Police Headquarters' where they bring their answers to get the clues.

The Ghost of the Séance

After a two-hour journey from London, Sherlock Holmes and Dr Watson drove up to the big manor house.

"So the main suspect in this murder is a ghost!" said Watson. "Is that really possible?"

"Of course not, Watson. We don't believe in ghosts. The murderer was human, and I am confident we will find him or her."

As they waited by the front door, Dr Watson read the short letter they had received that morning: "The doctor has confirmed that James Burton died of a heart attack caused by shock. He had a history of heart problems. But who scared him to death?"

"Well, Watson. They believe that it was the ghost of his daughter, Amy Burton, who killed him. She killed herself only two weeks ago after suffering from depression. Since then, strange things have been happening." Holmes looked up at the windows of the old house.

"Yes, it says here in the letter," said Watson, "James saw the ghost of Amy in the garden this week. Three days ago there was writing on the walls, in blood!"

"Yes," added Holmes, "He was so upset by the ghost that he called in a Scottish medium, Gordon McKay, to contact his daughter. Yesterday afternoon, they held a séance. Apparently, they spoke to Amy during the séance, but when it ended and they opened the parlour door, they found a note from Amy's ghost pinned to the back of the door with a knife."

"When James read the note he had a heart attack. They tried to find his medicine, but it wasn't in the usual drawer. Ten minutes later he was dead..."

"The murderer hid his medicine," said Holmes, calmly.

"Do you think so? How many suspects are there?"

"Well, four in total: The medium, Gordon McKay, James's second wife, Carol Burton, his youngest daughter, Rachael Burton, and the housekeeper, Meg."

Just then, the big front door opened and Meg stood before them.

"Ah, Mr Holmes, Dr Watson. Please come in."

As she led them to the main parlour, Holmes asked her: "Were you at the séance, Meg?"

"Oh yes. Everyone was. Only Amy's ghost could have left the note on the door." She stopped. "This is the parlour."

Holmes and Watson met the other guests in the parlour where the séance had taken place. Carol Burton was a French lady who had married James two years before. Gordon McKay was a big, quiet man who had been working as a medium for eight years. Rachael Burton was 25. After James divorced his first wife, 23 years ago, Amy stayed here with James, but the baby Rachael moved to the U.S.A. with her mother and has lived there ever since. She didn't visit often, but as soon as she heard about Amy's death, she came back to England.

After meeting all the guests, Holmes sat them around the dining table and said:

"I am certain that there is no ghost of Amy and that the killer is here in this room. I would like to interview each of you separately and examine the scene of the crime. In a few hours I hope to have a solution."

The Ghost of the Séance

Task instructions

Now you must try to solve the crime!

Your teacher has 14 <u>clues</u> that will help you to find the murderer. To win a clue, you have to decide if a sentence that the teacher will read out to you is right or wrong. Choose from the list below the clues that you think are most important and try to win them first. You do not need to get all the clues to solve the crime, but more clues will make it easier. You must name the murderer, say how they did it, why they did it, and <u>prove</u> it! Good luck!

The four suspects and the crime scene

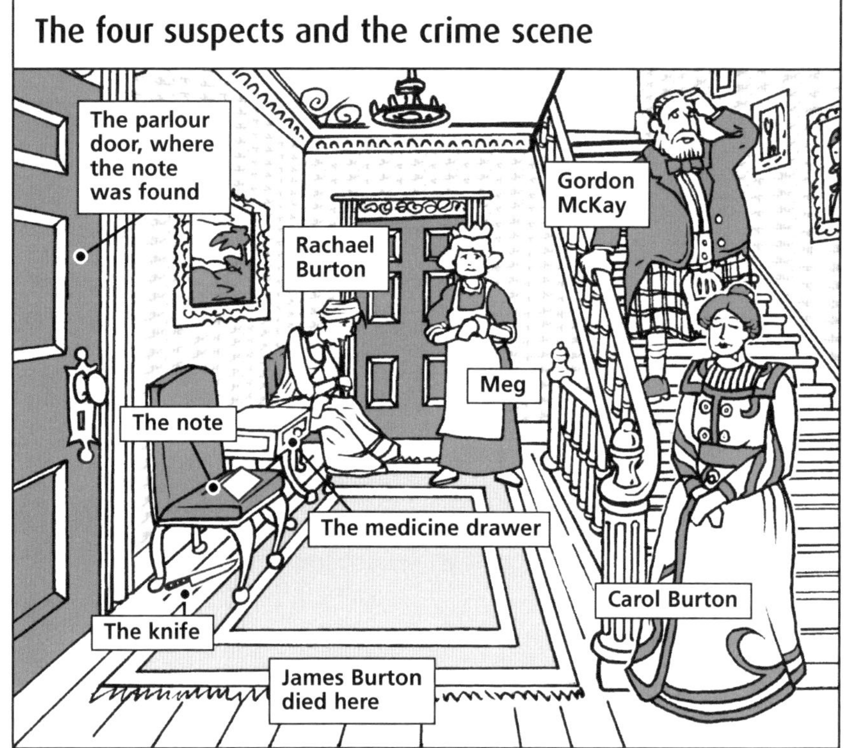

Clue list

Clue 1 The parlour
Clue 2 Who had a <u>motive</u>?
Clue 3 The note on the door
Clue 4 Interview with Meg, the housekeeper
Clue 5 The parlour door
Clue 6 The kitchen door
Clue 7 Interview with Rachael
Clue 8 The medicine <u>drawer</u>
Clue 9 Interview with Carol Burton
Clue 10 The garden
Clue 11 The knife
Clue 12 The body of James Burton
Clue 13 Interview with Gordon McKay, the medium
Clue 14 Help from Holmes

Vocabulary check

blood – red liquid (like water) inside your body
clue – information that helps you find the answer
confirm – say that something is true
criminal (*n*) – someone who breaks the law
depression – a continual feeling of deep sadness
drawer – container in a piece of furniture
examine – look at (carefully)
ghost – a dead person who comes back to life (*see picture*)
heart attack – very serious illness, can often kill
housekeeper – person whom you pay to cook and clean your house. They usually live with you.
human (*n*) – person
manor house – big, traditional old house
medium (*n*) – someone who can talk to the dead
motive – reason for committing a crime
murder (*n*) – when one person kills another on purpose
parlour – the living room in a big house
perfume – water or spray with a beautiful smell (for women)
pinned – attached
prove – show something to be a fact
reckon – think, believe
séance – a meeting in which a medium contacts the dead
scare (*v*) – make someone afraid / *scary* (*adj*)
slit (*n*) – a thin cut
stab (*v*) – to hit / cut someone with a knife
suspect (*n*) – someone who may be a criminal, but no-one knows
web – a net made by a spider to catch flies (*see picture*)
will – a document you write to explain what to do with your money, things etc. when you die
witness (*n*) – someone who sees a crime, accident, etc.

The Ghost of the Séance

Clue 1

The parlour

The parlour was typical for a house of that period. There were two doors out of the room. One opened into the hall and had the note on it. The other led into the garden. By the garden door there were two or three muddy footprints.

muddy (adjective) – dirty and wet *footprints*

Clue 2

Who had a motive?

"Holmes, don't we need a motive? Why did the murderer kill him?"

Holmes looked at Watson and nodded: "I've already checked that. I contacted James Burton's lawyer this morning. Although the contents of the will are secret, he told me that Carol, Rachael and Meg will all be a lot richer now he is dead, and that James did not keep the will locked away. He often talked about it with all of them."

"And the medium has no motive?" Watson asked.

"No money motive." Holmes said and walked off to look again at the scene of the crime.

motive – a reason for doing something, especially committing a crime.
lawyer – Lawyers are experts on the law. Sometimes they defend criminals in court.
will – a document written by someone to explain what to do with their property, money, etc. when they die.

Clue 3

The note on the door

The paper was folded in quarters and slightly crumpled. A centimetre long slit was cut in the centre, but it was easy to read the message, printed in red ink:

*You drove me to my death.
Now I'm going to return the favor. You're going to the center of hell,
dear Daddy!*

The paper was from Carol's writing desk.

folded – bent to fit in a small space, like a pocket
crumpled – old and used like an old banknote
slit – thin cut made with a knife

Clue 4

Interview with Meg, the housekeeper

"Meg, did you leave the séance at any time?" Holmes asked.

"Yes, just once, to get some water for Mr Burton. I went into the kitchen and came back very quickly."

"And on your way back, did you see the note on the door?"

"No, but the door was open, so perhaps I didn't notice..."

"And did you leave the parlour before, or after Carol Burton?"

"Before, I think. She left just as I was coming back..."

"Thank you, Meg. That will be all."

Clue 5

The parlour door

There was a large cut in the door. Holmes examined it and saw that it had been made by two stabs of the knife, not one. Each stab was over two centimetres long.

stab – the action of pushing a knife hard into something

The Ghost of the Séance

Clue 6

The kitchen door

The door at the end of the corridor (behind Meg in the picture) leads to the kitchen and the back door. When it is opened it creaks loudly.

creak – the sound an old door makes when it is opened, often slowly

Clue 8

The medicine drawer

The drawer was empty except for a small thermometer. Two bottles of emergency medicine were always kept here. It was clear that the murderer had stolen them and hidden them, planning for the 'accident'. There was a lock, but no key.

Clue 9

Interview with Carol Burton

"Did you leave the séance at any time, Mrs Burton?" Sherlock Holmes asked her.

"No... I mean, I didn't go into the house. About half way through the séance I got nervous and went into the garden to smoke a cigarette. There's a door from the parlour into the garden."

"Yes, I've noticed." Holmes paused. "That would explain the mud on the parlour floor. And how long were you in the garden?"

"Only about ten minutes."

"And did anyone else leave the séance?" Holmes asked.

"Yes, Meg went to get James a drink. I left just as she came back."

"How often do you smoke?"

"About three to five cigarettes a day."

"Always in the garden?"

"Yes, James didn't like the smell in the house."

"Thank you Mrs Burton. That is all for now."

Clue 7

Interview with Rachael

"I feel so bad, Mr Holmes. I hadn't seen Daddy or Amy for a year... And now I've lost them both." A tear fell from her eye as she spoke.

"I understand this must be difficult for you... But we need to find out who did this crime," said Holmes. "Did you leave the séance at any time, Rachael?"

"No. But I was the first one to leave at the end. The séance had gotten me real nervous. I saw the note on the door. I was so shocked. I pulled the knife out and read it... I nearly fainted. I called the others. My father came first, took the note and read it. He fainted right away. Meg rushed to get his medicine, but it wasn't in the drug drawer."

"I see. And did anyone leave the séance?"

"Yes, first Meg went to get James a drink of water and then later Carol went for a smoke in the garden, which was weird as she usually only smokes in the evening." She looked at Mr Holmes, "I know that you reckon it was one of those two that killed him, but believe me – there was a ghost. I saw it."

"Thank you Rachael. That is all."

gotten (American English) – *got*
faint – to fall unconscious because you are ill
drug (American English) – *medicine*

Clue 10

The garden

Holmes and Watson went out of the parlour through the door that leads into the garden. To the left were a few trees and a bench and to the right was a path that led to the back door. The door was locked. Holmes noticed an old spider's web in the keyhole. Watson went over to the trees and found the medicine, Mr. Burton's heart pills.

a web

"Holmes, look. Anyone could have put them here," said Watson.

"Yes. But the important questions are: *Why here?* and *Why were they so easy to find?*"

The Ghost of the Séance

Clue 11

The knife

It was an ordinary kitchen knife, not very long, but quite wide. Meg said it was from the kitchen, but she didn't notice it had gone. She said she last used it the night before to prepare dinner. A slight smell of expensive French perfume came from it.

Clue 12

The body of James Burton

The body was examined by the doctor and then taken away before Holmes and Watson arrived. The doctor was in no doubt, the cause of death was a heart attack brought on by shock.

Clue 13

Interview with Gordon McKay, the medium

"Come in, Mr McKay, sit down and relax," said Holmes. "Now, between you and me, I do not consider you a suspect in this crime... so therefore you are a very important witness. Who wrote to you to organise the séance?"

"Mr Burton."

"And how did he get your address?"

"From his daughter, Rachael, I guess. I met her at a séance in America when I was over there two years ago."

"I see. And do you have the letter from James?"

"No... I'm not sure where it is. It just said that they wanted to get in touch with a dead daughter. In the séance, Amy came to me immediately. I'm not surprised she left that note... Believe me, Mr Holmes, there is no murderer, except for the ghost."

"It's still too early to decide. Who left the séance as it was happening?"

"Only Meg and Carol. We paused for a moment because James needed some water. He sent Meg to the kitchen. And then when she came back, Carol went for a cigarette."

Clue 14

Help from Holmes

"All right," Watson said. "Let's say that the ghost was someone wearing a costume. But do you think it was more than one of them?"

Holmes smiled and lit his pipe: "No. There is only one criminal. If you are planning a crime, you need to trust your partners. They didn't have any time or reason to work together. The wife, Carol, was new; the daughter, Rachael, had just arrived from America; the housekeeper hates them all, and the medium was a first-time guest."

Watson's eyes lit up: "Surely it wasn't the medium. James's murderer was probably the ghost, and the killer probably stole James's medicine before the crime. Gordon McKay doesn't know where it was kept."

"That is true, Watson" said Holmes, "but you can find ways to eliminate all of them..." Holmes smiled and turned to look at a portrait on the wall "Or you can do it another way. You can think about the sound."

"What sound?"

"Exactly. The sound that no-one heard."

costume – clothes that you wear to look like someone else (e.g. a clown, or fancy dress)
eliminate – remove or take away

The Ghost of the Séance

The solution

When all the suspects arrived in the parlour, Holmes began:

"Let's eliminate the impossible," he started. "The ghost was played by a woman, so that eliminates our Scottish friend. Plus, he didn't know the facts written out in the note."

"Right," Watson agreed.

"That leaves Meg, Rachael and Carol. All three women knew Amy and all had motives."

Of course, there are three pieces of obvious evidence that point to Carol being the murderer. The knife smelt of her French perfume, and the paper for the note came from her desk... But any good murderer can steal a little perfume or paper from an open room. And hiding the pills in the garden where Carol often smoked was another clever trick.

But the real murderer made two small mistakes. Look again at the note," he said. "The words 'favor' and 'center' are spelt in American English, not British English. Of course, there was another way to know that you are the murderer, Rachael." The other guests all gasped and turned to her. Holmes continued, "The noise the knife made when it hit the door."

Watson checked his notepad carefully. "But no one heard a noise, Holmes."

"Exactly. Stabbing the door would have made a loud noise, especially since it was stabbed more than once. The only explanation is that Rachael stabbed the door several hours earlier. Then, when she came out of the parlour, she took the knife and note from her pockets and pretended she'd just found them on the door. If you carefully measure the size of the slit through the piece of paper, you will find it's only 1 cm long. But both the stabs in the door are 2 cm long. You were clever, Rachael, but not clever enough. Dr Watson, send for the local police."

You drove me to my death. Now I'm going to return the favor. You're going to the center of hell, dear Daddy!

eliminate – remove or take away
evidence – objects or information that lead to the murderer
stabbing (v) stab – the action of pushing a knife hard into something

The Ghost of the Séance

The solution

When all the suspects arrived in the parlour, Holmes began:

"Let's eliminate the impossible," he started. "The ghost was played by a woman, so that eliminates our Scottish friend. Plus, he didn't know the facts written out in the note."

"Right," Watson agreed.

"That leaves Meg, Rachael and Carol. All three women knew Amy and all had motives."

Of course, there are three pieces of obvious evidence that point to Carol being the murderer. The knife smelt of her French perfume, and the paper for the note came from her desk... But any good murderer can steal a little perfume or paper from an open room. And hiding the pills in the garden where Carol often smoked was another clever trick.

But the real murderer made two small mistakes. Look again at the note," he said. "The words 'favor' and 'center' are spelt in American English, not British English. Of course, there was another way to know that you are the murderer, Rachael." The other guests all gasped and turned to her. Holmes continued, "The noise the knife made when it hit the door."

Watson checked his notepad carefully. "But no one heard a noise, Holmes."

"Exactly. Stabbing the door would have made a loud noise, especially since it was stabbed more than once. The only explanation is that Rachael stabbed the door several hours earlier. Then, when she came out of the parlour, she took the knife and note from her pockets and pretended she'd just found them on the door. If you carefully measure the size of the slit through the piece of paper, you will find it's only 1 cm long. But both the stabs in the door are 2 cm long. You were clever, Rachael, but not clever enough. Dr Watson, send for the local police."

You drove me to my death. Now I'm going to return the favor. You're going to the center of hell, dear Daddy!

eliminate – remove or take away
evidence – objects or information that lead to the murderer
stabbing (v) stab – the action of pushing a knife hard into something

The Ghost of the Séance: Right or Wrong Grammar?

(Intermediate – Upper intermediate sentences)

1 I can't come to the party tomorrow because I'm going out with an old friend.

2 What does your brother do for working?

3 When I will get home tonight, I will call you.

4 I have never been to Spain, although I went to Portugal two years ago.

5 On a plane you don't have to smoke, even in the toilets.

6 I am very tired because I have just gone shopping.

7 I haven't seen my brother since three months.

8 I went to the post office to buy some stamps and to post some letters.

9 You shouldn't be worried about doing mistakes when you speak English.

10 We ate most of the meat, but we couldn't finish all the rice.

11 I like living in London, but it is so big city.

12 These trousers are too big for me, aren't they?

13 I spent twenty minutes waiting for a bus this morning, and then three came along at once.

14 Nobody I knew couldn't help me.

Answers

1 RIGHT
2 WRONG ...brother do for a living?
3 WRONG When I get home tonight...
4 RIGHT
5 WRONG You mustn't smoke...
6 WRONG ...I have just been shopping.
7 WRONG ...brother for three months.
8 RIGHT
9 WRONG ...worried about making mistakes...
10 RIGHT
11 WRONG ...it is such a big city.
12 RIGHT
13 RIGHT
14 WRONG Nobody I knew could help me.

The Ghost of the Séance: Right or Wrong Grammar?

(Upper Intermediate – Advanced sentences)

1 The more tired I get, the more I make mistakes.

2 I'm not going to the party unless you come with me.

3 I'd rather you didn't touch anything, please.

4 My friend's putting me down while I'm looking for a new flat.

5 I think they haven't been invited to the party.

6 I haven't even got enough time to get my hair cut this week.

7 I've always avoided to work in a big office – I don't like the atmosphere.

8 You couldn't have hurt his feelings – he's very insensitive.

9 She doesn't want anything to do with us now she's dating a famous footballer.

10 I forgot calling my grandmother yesterday. I'm so angry – it was her birthday!

11 Let's stay in and watch TV, shan't we?

12 I tried to know the correct answer, but the teacher wasn't sure.

13 Could you make sure the door's locked before you go out?

14 Very few people get away with cheating in exams.

Answers

1 WRONG ...the more mistakes I make.
2 RIGHT
3 RIGHT
4 WRONG ...putting me up...
5 WRONG I don't think they've been...
6 RIGHT
7 WRONG ...avoided working in...
8 RIGHT
9 RIGHT
10 WRONG I forgot to call...
11 WRONG ...shall we?
12 WRONG ...I tried to find out the correct...
13 RIGHT
14 RIGHT

Topic Index

Grammar and Functions Index

TEAMWORK

Interactive tasks to get students talking

Written by Jason Anderson

Edited by Xanthe Sturt Taylor

Designed by Christine Cox

Artwork by Stephen Lillie

Photo research by Emma Bree

Photos by
Page 19: J. Henley / Corbis.
Page 30: Vicky Starnes / Keltic.
Page 60: RubberBall / Alamy.
Page 61: Medioimages, PIXLAND / Alamy.
Page 63: Visit London.
Page 69: Mary Evans Picture Library.
Pages 28, 42, 51, 73, 74, 75, 76: Hemera.

1. Auflage 1 6 5 4 3 2 | 2021 20 19 18 17

ISBN 978-3-12-501732-0